Master
AMATEURS

ALSO BY KIRA ASATRYAN

*Stop Being Lonely: Three Simple Steps to Developing
Close Friendships and Deep Relationships*

Master AMATEURS

HOW NONPROFESSIONALS ARE POISED TO DOMINATE THE FUTURE OF WORK

KIRA ASATRYAN

BASALT BOOKS

Copyright © 2019 by Kira Asatryan
All rights reserved.

No part of this book may be reproduced, or stored in a retrieval system, or transmitted in any form or by any means, electronic, mechanical, photocopying, recording, or otherwise, without express written permission of the publisher.

The interviews in this book have been edited for length and clarity.

Published by Basalt Books, San Francisco
www.masteramateurs.com

Edited and designed by Girl Friday Productions
www.girlfridayproductions.com

Design: Paul Barrett
Project management: Sara Addicott
Cover image © Shutterstock/vectortwins

ISBN (hardcover): 978-1-7330734-1-7
ISBN (paperback): 978-1-7330734-0-0
ISBN (ebook): 978-1-7330734-2-4
Library of Congress Control Number: 2019908417
First edition

For Husbando

CONTENTS

Preface ix

CHAPTER 1: Master Amateurs 1
CHAPTER 2: Imperfection 19
CHAPTER 3: Greed 39
CHAPTER 4: Personal Responsibility 59
CHAPTER 5: Freedom 77
CHAPTER 6: Diversity 97
CHAPTER 7: Anger 119
CHAPTER 8: Personality 139
CHAPTER 9: Love 159
CHAPTER 10: Curiosity 179
CHAPTER 11: A Master Amateur in Ten Metaphors . . . 201

Notes 213
Acknowledgments 223
Index 225
About the Author 233

PREFACE

You have picked up this book, *Master Amateurs*, and now you have a question. What is a master amateur? Well, I'll spend the next two-hundred-plus pages answering that question. So, for now, I ask you to ask yourself a different question. That question is, Am *I* a master amateur?

How can I know? you may think. In fact, it's quite easy to know if you are one.

Do you describe what you do for work in multiple ways? Do you have more than one career pursuit? Have you ever decided to go out and do something despite having no relevant qualifications? Did you go to school for something but now do something else? Do you imagine, someday, you might do *yet another* something else?

If you answered yes to any of these questions, you are a master amateur. You are probably also a freelancer, a contractor, a self-employer, a self-styler, a flex-timer, a boot-strapper, a side-hustler, a gig-economist, a hyphenator, or a hired gun. You are likely also a creator, a quitter, and a starter. *A self-starter.* And you know—because you've taught yourself—how to self-start again and again and again.

You have a kaleidoscopic career. You may have it out of necessity—because impermanence is the name of the game in employment these days. You may have it because love, as well as work, matters to you. Love of adventure, love of abundance, love of change, love of freedom, love of family.

For now, know this: just because you don't adhere to the "one job for one lifetime" maxim does not mean you are a dilettante, an imposter, a commitmentphobe, or a failure. You are adapting—faster than others—to the work environment of the future. You have, in fact, the first truly twenty-first-century specialty. You are an expert at being an amateur.

You are also part of an ancient, storied tradition. People hardly remember this nowadays, but amateurism is the original lauded specialty. It was the career path for those wise enough to make their love their work. You freelancers, side-hustlers, and boot-strappers are the continuation of that great tradition.

In this book, I'll tell you the true stories of successful working master amateurs—your contemporaries—to illustrate the modern amateur's special set of skills, motivators, and strengths.

You'll meet Forrest Mims III, the most widely read amateur technologist of the computer age; Sheila Wysocki, a stay-at-home mom turned criminal investigator who solved the twenty-six-year-old murder of her college roommate; Kabir Sehgal, a Wall Street executive by day and Grammy Award–winning music producer by night; Ben Schatz, a Harvard-educated civil-rights lawyer turned drag queen; and Dylan Avery, an amateur documentarian responsible for the first internet blockbuster film, to name a few.

I'll also sprinkle in tales of amateur exemplars from the deep and recent past. These will include names you'll surely know, like Thomas Edison, Frank Lloyd Wright, and Amelia Earhart. They'll also include lesser-known amateur exemplars like Luke Howard, the father of modern meteorology; Mary Anning, the greatest fossil hunter ever known; Clara Barton, the founder of the American Red Cross; and Grote Reber, the first-ever radio astronomer.

I hope that these stories, along with my interspersed commentary, inspire you to do what you love without restraint, embrace the ethos of *not knowing* and proceeding anyway, and become the best amateur you can be.

CHAPTER 1
MASTER AMATEURS

But still try, for who knows what is possible?
—Michael Faraday

If you can believe it, there was once a time in America when the most admired career to have was no career. Today, for better or worse, a career is a load-bearing pillar of an accomplished life. But a short two centuries ago, the most successful person was the *man of leisure*, who, having opted out of the rat race thanks to inherited wealth, indulged his interests as he pleased, mostly from his armchair, his library, or his estate grounds.

The nineteenth-century man of leisure (and he most certainly was a man) was sometimes a naturalist, other times an antiquarian or a horseman, but he was quintessentially none of these. He was rich. Because he was rich, society afforded him the ultimate luxury: to do whatever he wanted, productive or not, with each of his days.

One hundred years later, the industrial revolution having changed just about everything that could be changed in society, the man of leisure was no longer the archetype of success. The twentieth century saw the scales of esteem tilt away from the man-who-did-whatever to the *professional*.

The professional was the man (and by midcentury, she was the woman too) who most certainly earned money, but not from doing just anything. He made money from selling his expertise—an expertise gained over years of government-certified training and education. Expertise replaced land as the most lucrative possession one could have, and it proved to be an extra-potent possession because—unlike land—expertise and the professional, once merged, became one and the same.

The elite status of professionals as "the men and women who know things" still stands as we hunker down into the twenty-first century. But every once in a while, you hear of a person achieving wild success without having a single credential to her name. You may meet someone, at a holiday party or wedding, who's had accomplished careers in two or even three different industries. You can probably name five people right now who've circumvented the professional route entirely and have nevertheless achieved great things.

Are these flukes? Did these people get lucky? Could they not make up their minds and somehow rode that indecision all the way to the bank? If enough noncommittal, flighty people bounce around from one career to the next, some of them will succeed by accident, right? Perhaps. But I intend to challenge the assumption that these fluid careerists are products of an attention-deficit society, unable to focus on one activity long enough to turn it into a life's work.

There's something bigger at play here. The phenomenon of decidedly *unqualified nonprofessionals* garnering status, wealth, and thought leadership is not an accident or a fluke. It's the emergence of a new type of working man and woman yet to be named, who takes an ultramodern approach to crafting a career.

This new type of working individual crafts their career (albeit usually unconsciously) around a core understanding that we're entering the most unpredictable period of human existence. It's hard to know what the world will look like in ten years, let alone a hundred, and these individuals know that making a living in the future means being flexible. As a result, they hold fast only to an ethos of constant experimentation and change.

They eschew adherence to any one profession not because they're unmotivated but because they believe that twenty years from now, one profession will not be enough. They often forgo formal training and education entirely not because they're undisciplined but because they believe a curriculum created in the past won't adequately prepare them for what's to come.

They forge their own tangential, circular career paths, often oscillating between two or more traditional occupations. They invent whole industries so they themselves can work in them. They crossbreed multiple disciplines to create their own vocational mash-ups. They embrace hyphenated job titles and build empires out of side-hustles. When an acquaintance asks them how that project they're working on is going, they proudly proclaim, *I'm not doing that anymore!*

Since these like-minded individuals are scattered across every endeavor known to humanity, they don't yet know that they're a community. But they are a community, and every community needs a name. So, I've decided to call them *master amateurs.*

Despite each person's uniqueness, master amateurs have one thing in common. It's not a similar background or a shared future goal. It's a philosophy that goes something like this: It's good to try, even when you don't know what's going to happen. It's good to produce, even in the face of uncertainty. It's good to proceed, even when you'll walk without solid ground beneath your feet. This is the philosophy that shapes master amateurs' unusual careers and lives.

Ironically, it's in their very refusal to formally commit to any "real" profession that master amateurs develop their careers. But this does not make them apathetic. If they have one thing going for them, it's that they take their amateurism seriously.

As we'll see in this book, the rise of master amateurs is just getting started. Professionals still dominate the working world, but they're about to feel the pressure, both economically and philosophically, from this group of upstarts, autodidacts, commitmentphobes, reformers, and flamboyant imposters called master amateurs.

MASTERS OF AMATEURISM

I call this new community of nonprofessionals master amateurs because they are amateurs who, paradoxically, have an expertise—and that expertise is amateurism.

Let's talk about amateurism. Amateurism has meant different things to different people over the decades, the details of which I'll go into later. For now, understand that I use the term *amateurism* to mean the pursuit of an interest, activity, or goal despite a lack of relevant formal training or education. To most people, this lack of formal training implies a lack of some critical knowledge. So, in blunt terms, amateurism is doing something without really knowing how to do it.

This would describe someone who makes a documentary film without ever having taken a class in filmmaking, solves a crime without ever having worked in the field of criminal investigation, cracks a scientific mystery on their kitchen counter in their spare time, or finds a new celestial body in their backyard with a borrowed telescope.

In this book, I take the notion of amateurism further and propose that it, as defined above, is a vocation in and of itself. The pursuit of a goal sans qualifications is not only a vocation but a craft with skills, knowledge, and core competencies to be mastered just like any other. Those who do master the competencies of amateurism are master amateurs and are able to apply their expertise to a wide variety of disciplines. A true master amateur may make a documentary, solve a mystery, *and* troll the night sky.

Let's talk about what it means to be a *master*. A master is someone who's developed exceptional skills in an art or craft, like smithing blades, brewing beer, or building towers. It's a term that also implies practical knowledge—not just esoteric knowledge, not just theory, but knowledge applied to real situations. An architect learns physics not necessarily because it interests her but because it helps her design sturdier structures. A smith learns metallurgy not so he can ace a test but so he can forge better blades.

Masters don't just talk the talk; they walk the walk. When called upon, they produce. This nuance of the term applies to master amateurs as well. Every person interviewed for this book has applied their knowledge of amateurism to tangible projects that have had real-world consequences. They've started businesses, invented products, made discoveries, answered age-old questions, hung artwork in galleries, and put criminals behind bars.

Taken together, *master* and *amateur* create quite the oxymoron, describing a person who *doesn't know* and produces anyway. As you meet them, you'll see this is exactly who they are. They don't just tolerate not knowing, as most of us do; they love and embrace not knowing. One master amateur you'll meet later says she always aspires to be "the dumbest person in the room," because in that unsteady state, she feels she produces the best results.

While professionals are still the men and women who know things, master amateurs are the women and men who *don't* know things—and that's working pretty well for them. They are the brave fools we sometimes admire and sometimes disparage, who don't know what they're doing and do it anyway.

COMPETENCIES OF THE FUTURE

If amateurism is a craft, then it has to have core competencies and skills that can be applied to real-world situations, like any craft does. While there's a whole suite of skills that master amateurs acquire through the practice of amateurism—we'll unpack these as we hear their stories—the core competency of a master amateur is acting strategically on one's own initiative.

In other words, master amateurs excel at noticing their own impulse to do something, whether that be to compose a symphony, manufacture vegan skincare products, or champion a social cause. They then take that impulse—that initiative—and proceed to act on it, without letting a lack of tactical know-how get in the way. A master amateur may know practically nothing about how proper historical research works, for example, but if she feels compelled to investigate an age-old mystery, she'll get started and figure out what she needs to know along the way.

This leads right into the second most important skill of amateurism: independent learning. In order to execute their vision, most master amateurs learn what they need to know in an informal, ad hoc manner. They gather information and resources using the "just-in-time" principle, meaning they'll learn what they need to know when they need to know it and not before. They learn what they need to know through hands-on experience, trial and error, communities of online and offline peers, and independent research.

This is certainly a haphazard way to learn, and most master amateurs freely admit that they don't have the depth of knowledge that single-subject experts have (like doctors, lawyers, or academics). Even a master amateur who, for example, starts a business to streamline legal billing will not know a fraction of what a lawyer knows about law. If looked at in a negative light, one could argue that because master amateurs lack a structured, monitored education, they know just enough to be dangerous.

That's a fair concern, and it's one we'll return to throughout this book. But there's a method to the madness here. Most master amateurs avoid gaining an encyclopedic knowledge of any one subject *on purpose*, because they believe it's a waste of time, given the trend toward decentralization of knowledge. Meaning, as knowledge lives more and more online, accessible (at least in theory) to anyone, it's inevitable that it'll live less and less within individual people. Master amateurs assume that people won't be the world's main repository of knowledge in the future, so many of them choose to invest their time elsewhere.

The same is true for technical skills. It's rare to find a master amateur who's recently taken up learning an advanced technical skill like operating a DSLR camera or a sonogram machine. They avoid this intentionally because, in the same way knowledge is becoming stored inside the internet, skills are becoming stored inside the tools themselves. Both knowledge and skills are becoming one with technology. For example, we can expect that within a decade, self-driving cars will make obsolete much of the human-based knowledge and skills currently involved in driving.

There is one major exception to the "master amateurs don't learn technical skills" rule, and that's learning to code. Many do invest in learning programming skills because it's one of a handful of ways to make an idea tangible, and that has great worth to someone who's building their career out of their own ideas.

So, what are master amateurs learning if they're not learning everything there is to know about a certain subject matter or acquiring advanced technical skills? They're learning how to best harness the tools, technologies, libraries, and mediums available to them. They're learning *how to learn*. Instead of trying to become a library of information himself, a master amateur learns to utilize the information already available to him. He knows that information is ever increasing, and he expects himself to be the agent who shows up and does something with it.

These two behaviors—acting on one's own initiative and learning how to learn—lay the foundation for a whole suite of other abilities that master amateurs get great at over the course of their careers. These include adapting to new environments, seizing opportunities, recruiting collaborators, experimenting and iterating, becoming comfortable with *good enough*, working hard without a guaranteed reward (like a paycheck or a degree), and ultimately, developing ease with constant change and perpetual resets.

These are not just skills that amateurs need to get great at to become masters; these are skills we should all be getting better at. These are the core competencies of the future. As the world gets smaller and changes happen faster, we could all stand to learn how to recognize a need and then figure out what's necessary to know how to address it. We could all learn to throw out our perfectionist tendencies and *just try something* without the fear-based need to know exactly how it'll turn out.

Since they are ahead of the curve in our increasingly unpredictable world, master amateurs will soon have the most desirable skill set of all: the skills of survivability despite constantly starting from scratch.

Even if you belong to the secure world of the professionals, the walls around your kingdom are crumbling. Single-subject experts can no longer interact only with peers and students; they, too, need to engage with the wider world to survive. This engagement is blurring a once-distinct line between professionals and everyone else—a line that we can expect to get only blurrier and not clearer as time goes on.

The promise of the professional was that he'd work from solid ground—he'd stand on a mountain of proven facts and tried-and-true techniques. His opinions would be grounded in verifiable realities. But what happens when the ground gives way and the mountain erodes? We master the skills needed to build on sand, walk through mud, and catch the sun while it's high.

TWO ROADS DIVERGED IN A WOOD

So far, we've portrayed the amateur as a self-taught adaptation expert. But it's important to understand the fraught legacy of the amateur, who has been at times indistinguishable from the professional, at other times the standard-bearer of good work ethic, and at other times a scourge upon otherwise reputable industries.

During the mid-1800s—the heyday of the man of leisure—there was no meaningful distinction between amateurs and professionals. Most everyone had their means of making money, and then they had their intellectual pursuits—science, literature, and the like. It was rare for anyone to make a living off their intellectual pursuits (one big exception being clergymen), so the idea that some people deserved to be paid for knowledge work and others didn't hadn't yet entered the public consciousness.

In fact, during this period, those who had more amateur tendencies were held in higher regard than those who leaned professional. Most people considered it noble to pursue an activity out of sheer love of it without the expectation of payment in return. The amateur actually had the *best* reason for working: he enjoyed it. The highly regarded man of leisure and the amateur overlapped in their motivation: they didn't do things because they had to; they did things because they wanted to. A remnant of this fleeting moment of positivity toward amateurs remains in the name's Latin roots—*amator*, "lover of."

But by the end of the nineteenth century, most industries that today have distinct professional and amateur tracks were starting to splinter. The rift in most disciplines formed out of fundamental differences in motivation. The proto-amateurs participated in an activity because they enjoyed it. The proto-professionals participated because, as they saw it, society needed them to.

Nowhere is this truer than in the history of botany. In mid-nineteenth-century America and Britain, one of the most popular pastimes was the collection, preservation, and organization of plant species. People of all income and status levels participated in what we would now consider botanical research, with no divisions among participants. Each one shared his specimens and notes with friends, neighbors, and anyone who asked. It was a hobby for all—something to do on a nice walk in nature.[1]

But by the end of the century, the first fissures between those who became the "botanists" and those who became the amateurs were forming, primarily because of motivational differences. The proto-professionals worked with plants because they wanted to further the field of natural science. They saw science as something bigger than themselves and felt compelled to contribute, however infinitesimally, to something of great importance.

The proto-amateurs, on the other hand, worked with plants as a means of self-improvement and personal discovery. They saw the gathering of plants, though effortful, as something that was good for them. It got them outdoors, it connected them with nature, and to some, it brought them closer to God. It was an upright, enriching use of their time. And that was it.

This difference introduces a couple of questions about amateurs, and master amateurs in particular, that we'll return to throughout this book: Are amateurs fundamentally more self-centered than their professional counterparts? Are professionals willing to sacrifice some personal pleasures for the sake of something more important? Are amateurs out for themselves while professionals are working for a greater good?

If you ask the average professional, he'll tell you (in not such direct language) that he's a serious contributor to a serious endeavor—an endeavor that matters, like science, medicine, law, business, or education. He'll tell you that he doesn't always work because he wants to; he works because he feels obliged to help society at large. He'll tell you that he puts up with a lot of grief to help his clients, customers, or patients. Yes, he gets rewarded for it, but it's only fair considering all he's given to his field of work and to his community.

This is, ironically, not that different from how a master amateur would describe himself. There's one important difference, though: a master amateur would not describe himself as *obliged* to do anything; he doesn't feel the need to repay some latent debt to society. Instead he's motivated internally, not externally, to work on this or that. In this sense, master amateurs are definitely self-centered. They're motivated from the self *out*. They often want to help others, but their own self is never far behind.

Let's go back to the botanists. The proto-professionals and the proto-amateurs had a difference in self-conception by the end of the nineteenth century. A difference in self-conception doesn't matter all that much until it has practical implications, which eventually it did. That breaking point—the functional rupture between the amateurs and the professionals—came at the start of the twentieth century, when the professional botanists, now backed by universities, stopped sharing their specimens with amateurs.

In other words, there came a moment when access to the basic building blocks of the discipline contracted. Access became limited, restricted. Certain people were able to keep practicing the discipline, and others were not. This meant that only some people, quite literally, held the keys to the kingdom. First, the proto-professionals developed a monopoly of access. Then, in short order, the fully formed professionals found that they had, as sociologist Magali Sarfatti Larson put it, a "monopoly of competence."[2]

In botany, the break came because of access to plant specimens. In astronomy, it came because of access to high-powered telescopes. In neuroscience, it stands to reason that the break came because of access to the labs where experiments were taking place. Whatever the discipline, the moment access is offered to some and denied to others, what was once one path splits into two.

ESTABLISHMENT OF THE ARMCHAIR

This is a good moment to note the critical role played by the modern university in the divergence of amateur from professional. Today, we know universities to be places of serious learning, where people learn not just what interests them but also the dry, boring, difficult stuff they need to succeed. It's always played another role too: that of the mechanism limiting access to "serious" learning to a select few.

Suffice it to say that getting into college is not an even playing field. It was an even more uneven playing field when the proto-professions were emerging. Wealthy white men decided what (and who) belonged in a university. Even today, if everyone were admitted into a certain academic program, it would lose its prestige. And a student who's been admitted into said academic program can't learn certain material without learning other material first. Limitation is woven into the fabric of the modern university as much as opportunity is.

But remember, before the invention of the modern university, serious learning was something an adult did almost exclusively at home or, like the early botanists, in nature. Anyone could explore nature, but the money and resources needed to perform experiments and publish results, to house libraries of texts and vaults of specimens, was beyond the capacity of individual people. The groups who made it into universities were afforded a sweeping advantage over everybody else.

An example of this can be seen in the history of history. Back in nineteenth-century Britain, the three disciplines we now know as history, archaeology, and antiquarianism had no clear boundaries among themselves. The study of primary historical texts (history), the excavation of historical sites (archaeology), and the collection of historical texts and artifacts (antiquarianism) overlapped to a degree that if you participated in one, you participated to some extent in all three.

But only history and archaeology survive to this day as legitimate professional fields. So, what happened to antiquarianism? The short answer: it never made it into the university system.

History was the first of the three to claim superiority. According to self-styled historians of the time, archaeologists were treasure hunters and grave robbers, and antiquarians were backcountry hoarders, little better than coin collectors. Only historians studied history with seriousness and rigor, and to prove it, they pled their case to the administrators at Oxford and Cambridge. Britain's ancient universities agreed, making history the first academic "study of the past" to exist separate from classicism. History became an independent course of study, and a few graduating classes later, it became a profession.

Archaeology followed suit a few decades later. The professional archaeologists kicked out the treasure hunters and—spearheaded by one of the discipline's founding fathers, Pitt Rivers—implemented scientific techniques for excavating sites and handling artifacts. The remaining "real" archaeologists were welcomed into universities, and the discipline became an independent course of study soon after.

Antiquarianism, however, never pulled off this transition. It never laid down the track, through standardized academic coursework, to becoming a profession. As British historian Philippa Levine described it, "No officially sanctioned training aimed at producing antiquarians was ever a serious consideration."[3]

Antiquarians were left behind, forever to be known as the amateur version of the other two—the "armchair historians" and "armchair archaeologists" we know today.

When professionals started jockeying for prestige through the mechanism of restricted access, the two roads—amateur and professional—forever diverged. Since then, *amateur* has meant little more than "not professional"—shorthand for "not up to par" or "not legitimate." While master amateurs represent a hopeful, positive vision of the future of work, it's important for any community to remember its past. So, let's not forget that for the last hundred or so years, an amateur was just about the worst thing you could be.

FAILURES, DABBLERS, DILETTANTES, AND FRAUDS

Over the course of the twenty-first century, the amateur has worn many faces, most of them not pretty. He's been the insubordinate who undermines a legitimate enterprise. He's been the illegitimate rival—the one who steals business from the rightful professional based on false promises. He's been the charlatan, the snake-oil salesman, the master manipulator. He's been the half-hearted dabbler—the one without enough talent or commitment to compete on the same level as the professional.

He's been a dilettante, a *fake* professional, a fraud.

Most often, he's been a nobody, really.

That's because, if asked, most people would define an amateur as simply *not* something else. A holistic healer is *not* a doctor. A mediator is *not* a lawyer. When I worked for a period of time as a relationship coach, I was considered *not* a therapist. Instead of having a discrete meaning of its own, amateurism has been defined in the negative. As the editors of the book *Amateur Media: Social, Cultural and Legal Perspectives* noted, amateurs have long been considered little more than *not* their "normative opposite."[4]

Is it any surprise that a term defined in the negative would take on a negative connotation?

But here's the kicker. There's no real definition of a *professional* either. Sociologists generally agree that a "line of work" becomes a profession when it has a standardized sequence of education, training, and qualifying exams, and a person is a professional when they've met those standards. But this definition doesn't apply to highly subjective professions like sports and entertainment, and it doesn't take into account the common notion that one exits amateur status as soon as she starts getting paid for her work.

Sociologist Julia Evetts perhaps defined *professionhood* as best anyone could, by simply saying that a line of work is a profession when it has a status quo, and a person is a professional when he or she has met that status quo.[5]

This definition creates an unflattering pickle for the amateur. If an amateur is just not a "professional," and a professional is someone who's met the status quo, then an amateur is nothing more than someone who's not met the status quo. That's a sour, nonsensical way to categorize people, and it accounts for much of the negativity thrown at amateurism for the last century. If that were all there was to it, we might as well call amateurism the art of failing, or the art of being worse.

The professional paradigm insists that it's important to envision amateurs in this negative light because if an amateur succeeds, she's subverting a precious status quo—a status quo to which countless professionals have yoked their identities and lives. Someone who hasn't met the status quo *should* fail, right? If she *doesn't* fail, that calls into question the importance of maintaining the status quo in the first place, right?

Right.

So, here's the reality. Many amateurs are *not* failing. A great number of self-described amateurs are making meaningful contributions to the world as well as accruing wealth, status, and thought leadership in traditionally professional endeavors. You will meet many of these successful amateurs right here in this book. They have a hopefulness and vibrancy we haven't seen since before the establishment of the armchair. They are our emerging leaders—the women and men who don't know what the future holds yet can't wait to take us there.

The era of the lifelong career is over, and these individuals who choose a life of perpetual novicehood—these master amateurs—show us how to prosper in a post-professional world, without dependence on status quos. Amateurism is the expertise of the future, and I predict that, not so long from now, professionals will look to amateurs to teach them how to begin again.

ABOUT THIS BOOK

The majority of this book will be dedicated to telling the true stories of real master amateurs. The first half of each chapter will profile a contemporary master amateur working today and succeeding in their own way (these profiles are based on interviews I conducted throughout 2017 and 2018). The latter half of each chapter contains mini-profiles of legendary amateurs from the deep and recent past. There will be names you'll recognize, like George Washington and Julia Child, as well as names you probably haven't heard, like Janet Stephens, LeeAnne Walters, and Grote Reber. There will also be some cautionary tales along the way.

My primary goal with these profiles is to understand, on a personal level, who master amateurs are. Where did they come from? What are their methods? What motivates them? Why did they decline, or avoid, conventional occupations?

Does criticism of their unusual career choices ever get to them? Does a lack of objective standards ever get to them? Does their own actual ignorance ever get to them?

And, most importantly, what do they have to teach us?

From their stories, I'll attempt to distill the qualities that make for a successful master of amateurism. Each chapter focuses on a particular quality, and you're free to jump around to whichever quality interests you the most. I believe a few readers will be drawn to the master amateur's bombastic iconoclasm and will aim to take on every trait. My hope is that every reader will find a few underrepresented qualities to strengthen within themselves.

I should also say that I intend to be fair in my portrayal of master amateurs. I want to shine a light on their particular type of greatness, but I'll also call them out when they're being problematic. And I'll reveal my bias up front: I consider myself a master amateur, and I think I'm pretty cool, so by extension I think they're pretty cool too.

Whether you fear master amateurs, dismiss them, disparage them, desire to become one, or realize from reading this that you already are one, you're about to get up close and personal with the most knowledgeable novices you'll ever know.

CHAPTER 2

IMPERFECTION

Perfect is the enemy of good.
—English aphorism

I WANT TO DO ALL THE THINGS

The red Nissan serving as my Lyft today parks at an incline on Harrison Street between First and Second. I pop out and hike the sloped entrance to Terra Gallery & Event Venue in San Francisco. We're in the heart of SOMA, just a few hills up and down from where I live. Upon entering the cavernous venue space, a baby-faced man with windswept hair guides me to pick up my badge at the registration desk. He's wearing 500 Startups' go-to volunteer garb: an electric-blue T-shirt on which *South Park*'s Cartman screams, *"Respect my authoritah!"*

I've come to Demo Day—the day when all startup founders in 500 Startups' accelerator program pitch their ideas to investors—to find someone who's achieved legendary status in my own mind. It's not Dave McClure, the now-disgraced creator of 500 Startups, nor Christine Tsai, the woman who took the helm after Dave fell into "sexual misconduct" waters.

No, I'm looking for a young woman who might be the most masterful amateur of all time.

I've started my search for master amateurs in Silicon Valley because it's one of the few places where people regularly achieve wealth, power, and influence despite having little formal training in their particular job functions. This is true even in the most critical roles. Only 24 percent of startups valued at over a billion dollars have even one founder with an MBA.[1] The vast remainder of startup founders and executives are software engineers who learn how to run a business through peer-to-peer advice and trial and error. Software engineers as a group are notoriously autodidactic; one recent study showed that 69 percent of software engineers consider themselves to be self-taught.[2]

I grab my badge and scan the perimeter of the space. It's lined with booths—twenty-seven to be exact—each serving as a meet-and-greet station for a startup looking for investment. I have to scan slowly, as the majority of attendees are wearing small variations of the same outfit: a cowboy-blue button-down, dark-washed jeans, and a smart brown belt. Some throw on a smartwatch for flair.

As I'm searching for an amateur in a haystack, I'm struck by the symbolism of the Silicon Valley uniform. It's rare to see such a lack of sartorial braggadocio. It's there under the surface, of course—the stratification of wealth. But on the surface, everyone looks to be of the same status, from the fat-and-happy investors to the ramen-fed founders. The amateurs and the professionals are far from easily distinguishable in the startup world. Everyone has an iPhone; no one has a Rolex.

I spot her. Her name is Charu Sharma, and she's the founder and CEO of Next Play, one of the startups gunning for investment today.

I, however, first knew her as a film producer.

Back in 2016, a friend of mine took me to a local coding school to see a documentary about female tech entrepreneurs called *Go Against the Flow*. Charu produced the film. She presided over a panel discussion of well-known female entrepreneurs at the screening and remarked, offhandedly, that *Go Against the Flow* had been screened all over the world, from "the Empire State Building in New York to the National Gallery of Singapore."

Charu stuck with me.

A few months later, I received an email from 500 Startups announcing their newest batch of incubated companies. There again was Charu, this time credited as the founder and CEO of Next Play—a startup building a mobile app to improve intra-company mentorship programs through artificial intelligence.

Who is this person? I wondered.

I closed the email from 500 Startups and Googled her. One of the first hits was Charu's Amazon author page. *She's an author too?* I puzzled. *As well as a film producer . . . and a tech founder?*

That's a lot.

I scrolled down to her author biography. I read the first paragraph and, unable to control my reaction, shouted out, "What?"

"Charu Sharma is an award-winning entrepreneur, explorer and author based in Silicon Valley," it read. "With 5 National Awards, expeditions to all 7 continents, over 600 stage shows, and two startups, this prodigy was enlisted as a 'Power Woman' alongside such notables as Oprah Winfrey, Sonia Gandhi, and Melinda Gates by Youth Incorporated magazine in March 2012."[3]

She can't be more than twenty-five years old! I thought. A little more Googling revealed she was born in 1992, making her (at the time) twenty-five years old.

How, I wondered, *could someone that age have done so many things?* If these were factual, on-record accomplishments, how did she manage them all? She must be a true master of amateurism. An *amateur savant,* even. She must be someone who's able to pick up any task and—without training or qualification—make it happen.

I needed to know more.

So, the day after I approached her at Demo Day, Charu agreed to meet up with me for coffee at the Creamery in SOMA. She wears lavender jeans and an olive-green army jacket, her long, lustrous hair pulled back in a loose ponytail. Instead of sitting at a table, she decides we should sit next to each other on a bench. She swivels to face me and arranges herself cross-legged, all warm and smiling.

Her warmth is inviting. But it makes me realize I don't have a polite way of asking the question I want to ask, which is: *So, you're a total amateur at everything you do, right?*

I cough.

"Tell me about yourself," I offer instead.

༄ ༄ ༄

Charu Sharma was born on March 24, 1992, in Jaipur, India. At the age of six, her family moved to Mumbai. Her father was a prominent interventional cardiologist at Bombay Hospital and Medical Research Centre. Despite his professional success, Charu's family lived in a cramped hostel on the research center's campus. Her mother, Neha, was by Charu's account tremendously driven and intelligent, but because of Indian social norms, she never had a career. She was a housewife.

In describing her childhood, most of Charu's memories revolve around her mother pressing her to succeed. "My mother pushed me so hard," Charu recalls. "I had two black belts, one in karate and one in tae kwon do, by the time I was fifteen." Neha encouraged Charu to be ambitious and to take on any challenge that interested her. Neha believed that not only could Charu do whatever she wanted to do but she should do *everything* she wanted to do.

Immediately upon hearing this, Charu's jam-packed resume makes a little more sense to me. If Neha could not have any career, Charu seems determined to have *all the careers*.

In 2010, Charu immigrated to the US on a scholarship to study economics and physics at Mount Holyoke College. I ask her why she left India, and she, in no uncertain terms, says it was to escape the expectation that women should not work. With that expectation lifted, Charu was free to do *all the things*. In addition to her studies, she started two technology-based companies out of her dorm room and spent her spare time exploring the world on Semester at Sea voyages (these voyages account for the "expeditions to all 7 continents" resume item).

"I know it seems like I did a lot," Charu comments on this period of ravenous *doing*, "but I wasn't thinking at all about my resume during college. I was just curious about everything and wanted to do everything."

Now, I'm the one who's curious. "When you're doing a little bit of everything," I ask her, "how do you know enough about any of the things to do them well? I mean, in a really short period of time you've started businesses, built a mobile app, written a book, filmed a documentary—"

Charu stops me. All of these projects are more similar than they are different, she says. Each requires learning just enough, tactically, to be able to get your point across. But the goal is not to make any one of them perfect, she explains, because ultimately they're just means to an end.

"The projects are just mediums," she tells me. "They're just different ways to get your point across."

"But when you do everything, don't you kind of do nothing?" I press her.

"That's not how I think about it," she responds. "I wasn't trying to be a professional writer or even a published writer when I wrote my book. I wasn't trying to be a filmmaker when I made my film. I'm mission-driven. I just wanted to further my mission in any way possible—through any medium possible."

"What's your mission?" I ask.

"To create systems that enable equal access for everyone."

I'll come to learn through my series of interviews with master amateurs that Charu Sharma has a prototypically amateur mind-set about work. To her, work is about *doing* something; it's not necessarily about *being* something. A medical student works to *become* a doctor. A law student works to *become* a lawyer. But an amateur will work to make a film, for example, and not care at all about being a filmmaker. She will conduct a survey without wanting to be a researcher. She'll start a business and have no interest in being an entrepreneur. For masters of amateurism, their identity is separate from their efforts.

Once Charu describes her personal mission to me, she turns inward for a moment. She starts talking, unprompted, about a TEDx talk given by Reshma Saujani, founder of Girls Who Code. The talk is titled "Teach Girls Bravery, Not Perfection." In it, Reshma asserted that men get ahead in society because boys are raised to be brave, while girls are raised to be perfect. From the stage, Reshma pleaded with her audience: "I need each of you to tell every young woman you know . . . to be comfortable with imperfection."[4]

"I know so many people," Charu confides in me, "who do not want to share what they're working on unless it's perfect. Most of my friends want to learn something really well before they start doing anything with it."

But this is a self-imposed limitation, Charu implies, that holds people back from doing everything they want to do.

Especially women.

Most especially young women.

Charu's breakthrough came, she explains to me, when she started publicly sharing her projects *before* they were great. She started sharing her creations knowing full well they weren't excellent yet. This is, in a sense, her methodology for getting *all the things* done. She starts on a project, and once it's decent—workable, passable—she'll put it out in the world, gather feedback, and improve it over time. She's done this enough times that now she's perfectly comfortable stamping her name on something that's just *good enough*.

It sounds small, but I find this to be Charu's most impressive strength. It's the source of her vocational power and stamina. It's the thing she can teach us all: don't *not* do something you want to do because you fear it will only be *good*.

In most cases, good is enough. A lot of the time, good is great.

Good is also a potent challenge, in a way, to professional elitism. A professional filmmaker might look at Charu's work and say, "My film is better than yours." No doubt Charu would happily respond, "It is! But my film is good enough."

"Has anyone ever straight-out told you you're not qualified to do something?" I ask Charu.

"All the time!" She laughs. "I just genuinely don't care about that. Back in India, I was always competing and achieving, competing and achieving. So, when I came to the US, I decided just to *learn*."

It's like a cool breeze settles over us when she says this.

"Anyone can just go learn *anything*."

To someone like Charu, who grew up in a world equal parts achievement and repression, where success and access are one and the same, I can see why she thinks this is the ultimate luxury. *Just go learn anything. Just go do everything.*

"Are you ever scared?" I ask, mostly to myself.

"What do you mean?" she replies.

"When you do a little bit of everything . . . does the lack of security ever scare you?"

"No," she states. "I find security scary because security, to me, equals being complacent."

For reasons known only to her, this reminds Charu of her father, the cardiologist. "He was one of the most brilliant intellectuals I've ever known," she tells me. "But he wasted fifteen years of his career being someone's assistant . . . and the only reason was he was scared to let go and start an independent practice. He was scared to try."

Her father did everything right, in her summation, except for one thing. He feared trying without knowing what would happen. He held himself back out of fear that his individual efforts might be lacking. And this, to Charu Sharma, is the real thing to be feared.

A MILLION LITTLE DREAMS

One of the master amateur's greatest strengths is her ability to tolerate the severely lacking first version of her creation, which often lays bare her deepest fears, anxieties, flaws, and imperfections. Looking at your own work is like looking into a mirror—an unnerving experience if you don't love what you see.

When you take on a project without the security of an official seal of approval, you'll be greeted at once by the personal demon you wrestle with most. It may be an exasperating habit (like procrastination), a counterproductive tendency (like rage or impatience), or simply the litany of things you don't know yet. The delta between where you are in the beginning and The

Dream—an excellent contribution to humanity—can seem so wide at first it feels stupid to try.

This is a quandary: the desire for greatness is surely there; otherwise why bother, especially if bothering requires a sacrifice of income, status, security, or community? Why volunteer to struggle, fall short, and produce something deficient? Who wants to spend a couple of years, at least, making rookie mistakes? At the same time, common sense tells us that nobody's brilliant in the beginning, no project starts completed, and nothing is born grown up.

One big advantage professionals have over amateurs is that professionals are, for a set period of time, required to be infants. They are first students, then interns, residents, apprentices, or the like—all labels that imply their abilities are still in development. They're good enough to be at the stage they're at, but they're not perfect yet. They're in the oven, but they're not fully baked.

This is an advantage because it teaches professionals-in-training that it's normal to be bad at something before you're good at it. The novice is a novice through no fault or deficiency of his own—that's just where he's at. His work is subpar because he's new at it. That's not a reason to stop progressing.

But amateurs often take subpar initial performance as a reason not to continue. They think: *The fact that my work sucks is a good reason to stop trying, right? But I still want to try. So, what do I do?*

Some amateurs choose the path of not caring, meaning they work on a project without concern for how "good" it is. They do what they want, others' opinions be damned. This is a popular approach right now, but it has drawbacks. Not caring—a.k.a. indifference—is hard to keep in neat little containers. Cultivate enough indifference and it'll spill over onto The Dream. Get too good at not caring and suddenly you won't care about your project either. It's not easy to nurture passion and dispassion at the same time.

Instead, successful master amateurs care very much about very, very small things. They shrink the space between where they are now (let's say at "terrible") and where they want to be (let's say at "world-changing contribution to humanity") by placing finish lines all along the track. There's the big dream, and then there are teeny, tiny dreams all along the way. Some master amateurs have the over-the-top luxury of achieving a dream every single day.

A perfectionist might see "good" as about halfway to the end goal, or mediocre. But to a master amateur, "good" represents a million little dreams fulfilled. It means you've reached the end of the beginning and can begin again, this time better. From this perspective, it's easy to see why Charu happily promotes her just-good-enough creations.

This method may seem like psychological trickery, and it is. It tricks you into wanting to do something you don't want to do, which is to approach, examine, rethink, and incrementally revise a bad try.

Notice I didn't say "incrementally improve" a bad try. Improvement happens, but it's not a linear process. Oftentimes, you won't know in the moment whether a change you're making is an improvement. It may just be a change—an option, an experiment, an alternative, another try. But when every attempt is a success, there are a million little reasons to keep trying.

EDISON'S UPSIDE-DOWN WORLD

America's most prolific inventor, Thomas Edison, held 1,093 patents in his lifetime—the most patents ever registered to a single person. He's credited with inventing the phonograph (the first machine to record and reproduce sound), the motion-picture camera, the alkaline storage battery, and most famously, the incandescent electric light bulb. He also coined the standard American telephone greeting—"Hello!"—after convincing Alexander Graham Bell it was better than Bell's now-hilarious-sounding preferences: "Ahoy!" and "What is wanted?"[5]

Edison was a tenacious taskmaster with a rudimentary education and an unwavering conviction that he could invent anything—all he needed was a pile of junk and an army of assistants. Nearly all Edison's inventions required thousands of trials to get right, with the notable exception of the phonograph—the only invention he got right on the first try. Edison reportedly distrusted the phonograph for the rest of his life and refused to promote it because its invention had been suspiciously easy.

The invention of the light bulb, on the other hand, was not easy. Technically, Edison did not invent the electric light bulb (twenty-three others had produced light bulbs before him), but he made the first commercially viable one. Electric light would never work indoors until someone found a durable filament that could safely, softly illuminate a room for a substantial amount of time before being incinerated.

Edison and his assistants (described by George Bernard Shaw as a band of "liars, braggarts, and hustlers") burned over six thousand materials in their quest for the right filament, including platinum, celluloid, sewing thread, coconut hair, cardboard, cedar, and "cotton soaked in boiling tar," before landing on carbonized bamboo from Japan.[6] The thin bamboo thread successfully incandesced for twelve hundred hours before subliming in the electrical current. It became the standard material used in "Edison bulbs" for the next ten years.

Incredibly, Edison trumped the light bulb's record-breaking six thousand trials when working on one of his later inventions: the alkaline storage battery. According to his associate Walter S. Mallory, after more than five months, Edison and his team had "made over nine thousand experiments in trying to devise this new type of storage battery, but had not produced a single thing that promised to solve the question."[7]

Mallory, overwhelmed with pity for Edison, asked, "Isn't it a shame that with the tremendous amount of work you have done you haven't been able to get any results?" Edison bellowed, "Results! Why, man, I have gotten lots of results! I know several thousand things that won't work!"[8]

Thomas Edison was devoid of self-doubt, ruthlessly methodical, vaguely narcissistic, and taken to outsourcing the banalities of experimenting to others. He was not perfect, and "be self-confident to the point of delusion" is not the lesson here.

The lesson is: value every attempt. Edison may have been naturally unflappable, but he also gained strength by valuing every attempt. He held every try to be a precious jewel. The reward, for him, was synonymous with the effort.

A successful master amateur learns to live in Edison's upside-down world, where unsuccessful tries are successful and efforts that don't yield the desired results get celebrated. In Edison's world, sometimes you get an era-defining invention out of your efforts and other times you fill your personal treasury full of precious attempts.

EXPERIMENTS, PROTOTYPES, PIVOTS, AND DRAFTS

The notion that to make progress one must confront and rethink an initial failure is nothing new. Numerous industries have names for insufficient yet invaluable initial tries. In technology, for example, they're called prototypes. Edison would surely have called his attempts prototypes had he lived a few decades later.

Edison's intellectual scion and camping buddy, Henry Ford, made nineteen automobile prototypes (Models A through S) before producing the legendary Model T. James Dyson, inventor of the bagless vacuum cleaner, made 512 prototypes of his dual-action cyclone technology before it worked as he wanted. He, too, lived in an upside-down world: "We're taught to do things the right way," Dyson once said, "but if you want to discover something that other people haven't, you need to do things the wrong way."[9]

In science, trial and error (and then trial and error again) is called experimentation. One pioneer of scientific experimentation, Dutch businessman Antonie van Leeuwenhoek, ran countless experiments and handcrafted over five hundred magnifying lenses to answer a question that plagued him: What the heck are those specks in pond water?

A commercial merchant by occupation, Leeuwenhoek's contemporaries dismissed him as an amateur scientist and careless dilettante. But his steady pursuit of ever-more-powerful magnifying lenses made him the first person to observe and describe single-celled organisms. He's now the unquestioned father of microbiology.

In the 1970s, another amateur scientist experimented her way to a nearly indestructible building material. A fine artist by training, Patricia Billings started experimenting with reagents to harden plaster after one of her beloved swan sculptures fell to the floor and shattered. She spent the next eight years trying to re-create the hardened plaster used by Michelangelo and other Renaissance masters, only to succeed when she mixed gypsum, concrete, and a still-secret chemical catalyst.

When a fellow scientist noted the material was heat resistant as well as durable, Billings spent another eight years making her plaster fully fireproof. The material, known today as

Geobond, can resist a 6,500-degree blast from a jet engine and is the most widely used building plaster in the United States.

In the business of startups, a second try is called a pivot. Many culture-defining tech products are second or even third pivots. Instagram started life as a location-based iPhone app called Burbn (after the Kentucky whiskey, for no apparent reason). Twitter launched as a place to find and subscribe to podcasts. Flickr began as an online role-playing game called *Game Neverending*. Groupon began as a "social good" fundraising site to gather and organize volunteers.

On its first try, YouTube was a dating site with the unfortunate slogan "Tune In, Hook Up." Cofounder Jawed Karim recalled calling their platform a dating site simply because they didn't yet know what it was. "The whole thing didn't make any sense," he remembered.[10] It wasn't until users started uploading funny clips to the video section of the site that they realized they had a video platform.

As often happens after a creation has traversed the terrain from bad to good to world-changing contribution, the first iteration seems painfully, obviously wrong in retrospect. But you have to wonder: Without the thing that didn't make sense, would these creators have arrived at the thing that did?

In the craft of writing, the bad version that precedes the better version is called the first draft. First drafts are at once utterly humiliating, hilarious, painful, and essential. In his memoir, *On Writing*, Stephen King described his visceral reaction to the first version of *Carrie*, saying he wrote "three single-spaced pages of a first draft, then crumpled them up in disgust and threw them away."[11] Luckily, his wife, having found the pages in the wastebasket and read them, encouraged him to finish the draft. She wanted to know what happened next.

J. K. Rowling has also described her bewilderment at early versions of the Harry Potter books. *Harry Potter and the Philosopher's Stone*—the most innocent and fanciful of the installments—once opened with a gruesome scene in which Hermione's father finds the dead bodies of Harry's parents lying in the ruins of their apparently exploded house. "I can't remember now why I thought this was a good idea," Rowling has mused.[12] Her bewilderment at her own initial ideas is a testament to just how far she's come.

First tries are not all embarrassment and stupefaction, though. Women and men who've come far from their first try usually look back on it with appreciation as well. The beginning was hard and weird, but it was a necessary crucible to live through, and they're grateful to have done it (and to not be doing it now).

The thing is, master amateurs deal with a lot of beginnings and a lot of first tries—many more than professionals do. If your expertise is amateurism, you'll be starting over a lot. While it's easy to appreciate the endearing inadequacy of a first try when you're on your hundredth, the challenge for a master amateur is to bring appreciation into the present. In other words, a master amateur must look back with fondness on something *while they're actively working on it.*

They must bend time and space to see the value of a novice's work through an expert's eyes. They must travel through a type of amateur's wormhole, through which they can recognize the beauty of the beginning as if they were at the end.

THE REMEDY MUST COME THEREAFTER

In 1752, just before the start of the French and Indian War, the royal governor of Virginia appointed George Washington commander of the Virginia colonial militia. He had no military experience. He aspired to be a farmer, he liked mathematics, and he earned money as a land surveyor. But his unique talent for motivating cold, wet amateur soldiers in battle was paramount in the context of the impending war for independence.

Later in life, Washington's peers considered him the only choice for president of the United States, citing his unmatched leaderships skills (as we would call them today). The consensus was complete, making Washington the only president ever elected by unanimous vote. He balked at this but accepted the position anyway. "While I realize the arduous nature of the task which is conferred on me and feel my inability to perform it," Washington said at his inauguration, "I wish there may not be reason for regretting the choice."[13]

To be fair, all of America's founding fathers were amateur governors; Washington was no more or less amateur than the rest when it came to running a country. Lack of experience bothered some of them greatly and others not at all.

Washington was particularly needled by his own inexperience. He was no self-certain Edison. He was weighed down with self-consciousness and hyperawareness of his shortcomings. He worried that he'd misstep and set a bad precedent for future American leaders. He wished their government could be born into the world fully matured, but setting that wish aside, he set out to birth the American government as an infant.

When you're doing something new, it's semi-impossible to know if you're doing it right. This was never truer than during the drafting of the Constitution. Washington presided over the Constitutional Convention of 1787, during which legislators had to formally empower the federal government; otherwise the country risked splintering into state governments or falling to a foreign power. The dangers of not acting were imminent; they needed to get a mandate on the books, whether it be great, good, decent, or barely passable.

In a letter Washington sent to former governor of Virginia Benjamin Harrison, he seemed to think what they came up with landed somewhere between decent and good. Or good enough.

"I wish the Constitution which is offered had been made more perfect," Washington wrote, "but I sincerely believe it is the best that could be obtained at this time—and as a constitutional door is op[e]ned for amendment hereafter—the adoption of it under present circumstances of the Union is in my opinion desirable."[14]

Washington took consolation in the fact that the legislators "left the door open" for amendment to the Constitution in the future, a fact he reiterated in a letter to his nephew Bushrod:

> The warmest friends to and the best supporters of the Constitution, do not contend that it is free from imperfections; but these were not to be avoided, and they are convinced if evils are likely to flow from them, that the remedy must come thereafter; because, in the *present moment* it is not to be obtained. And as there is a Constitutional door open for it, I think the people (for it is with them to judge) can, as they will have the aid of experience on their side, decide with as much propriety on the alterations and amendments w[hi]ch shall be found necessary, as ourselves; for I do not conceive that we are more inspired—have more wisd[o]m—or possess more virtue than those who will come after us.[15]

When you're fighting for your independence, the decision to proceed with a good-enough start seems straightforward. When the consequences of not acting are dire, it makes sense to go with what you've got.

Today, most decisions, especially oblique decisions about whether to work on this project or that, are not made under such duress. But there are still consequences to not trying—not life-or-death consequences, but something similar to life or death of The Dream. A master amateur keeps his dream alive by enacting what he's got and embracing the promise of perpetual amendment.

GOOD ENOUGH

If you want to become a master of amateurism, develop a working relationship with *good enough*. It'll be the place from which you start again and again as you take on unprecedented work. As time chips away at the status quo, the line between perfect and imperfect will blur. This will paralyze those who need to be excellent before they can even get started.

Also, remember that good enough is not a standalone objective. Successful master amateurs couple good enough with constant amendment, experimentation, and inevitably, improvement. Without a commitment to look a lacking try in the eye and change it, good enough plays right into the amateur stereotype (as the one whose work is subpar). Instead, good enough is a starting line, and every step taken thereafter is a finish line—an achievement in and of itself.

One clarification to make before we move on: a master amateur's comfort with imperfection does not mean she's pro-imperfection. There's a principle in Japanese art called *wabi-sabi*, which says that flaws make a work of art great, that imperfections are required to make something beautiful.

This is not that. Most master amateurs would rid their work of shortcomings at once if they could, but they've learned from experience that that's not how things work. Master amateurs are not pro-imperfection; they just recognize that the desire for instantaneous flawlessness is a trap. It's a limiting belief that creates a cavalcade of reasons not to try.

So, successful master amateurs proceed knowing that nothing starts done. You might get lucky and get it right the first time, like Edison did with the phonograph. But in all likelihood, you'll end up being Edison with the light bulb or the alkaline battery. What's not thrilling about that?

CHAPTER 3
GREED

> *Greed is good.*
> —Yuppie slogan

A PRODUCT OF OUR TIME

"I am definitely a fraud. I've always been a fraud," Matt Monahan declares. He's someone who prides himself on a plexiglass-like transparency. "I'm as fake as it fucking gets, but I'm a product of our time. Our whole world, our whole environment is fraudulent. It's the paradigm we live in today." He pauses. "Anybody who says they're not fake is even more fake than I am."

Matt Monahan is the given name of The Most Famous Artist, an LA-based painter and muralist known for his blatant amateurism, lack of objective talent, and witty take on internet culture. He's garnered a monetary success that makes "serious" artists seethe. Once, a film crew doing an interview with The Most Famous Artist (TMFA for short) asked him to paint something so they could use it later as B-reel footage. "Being that I don't actually know how to make any art," TMFA mused, "this is going to be interesting."[1]

Over the course of his short, five-year career, TMFA has shown in over a dozen prestigious galleries and earned significant income selling simple, smart pieces of art that anyone could make. His early works were modified found objects—mostly ugly thrift paintings he found at flea markets. He'd take the flea-market painting and dip it in neon to create the impression the old painting was melting into something new. He'd black out parts of the painting to show how we censor our lives online. He'd spray-paint logos like those of Louis Vuitton or Nike across the painting to prove we'll buy anything associated with the right brand.

TMFA is entirely self-taught, but even that is overstating his credentials. He purports to not be able to paint (in the traditional sense) at all and has no interest in learning. He has thick, calloused skin owing to years of blistering criticism from the fine-art establishment, which at first ignored him completely, then derided him, then begrudgingly held him at arm's length.

At the same time, he has sore spots. He hears one criticism so frequently—that anyone could make his art—that he sells a T-shirt on his website blaring the words "Go fucking do it then." It's hard to know if he means it as a clapback, a pep talk, or both.

※ ※ ※

Before Matt Monahan was The Most Famous Artist, he was an ambitious, Stanford-educated advertising executive. In early 2013, he was founder and CEO of an advertising-technology company called AlphaBoost. The company had just raised $1 million from a top-tier venture-capital firm. To celebrate, he and a group of tech entrepreneurs took a self-described "geek trip" to the beaches of India. There, a fellow trip-goer filmed

Matt blackout drunk and naked—slurring his words, penis flapping in the subcontinental wind—and sold the footage to Gawker. In a mindless instant, Matt's advertising career was over.

"I became known as the drunk, naked founder," he reminisces. "So, I had to go back to the drawing board."

For the remainder of 2013, Matt holed himself up and pondered what, if anything, he'd learned from his time in advertising. He was searching for some scrap of knowledge he could leverage in the new career he'd now have to create.

A couple of advertising principles stuck with him. First, that the best products to sell have high profit margins—meaning they can be sold for much more than they cost to make. These high-margin products are usually visual and have some clever component that makes people want to talk about them without consciously knowing why.

He ruminated on this, and one day it dawned on him. The best industry to enter, based on these criteria, was obviously art. "The best product I could sell given my skill set was art," he tells me. "Without the ad-tech experience, it never would have occurred to me to become an artist."

I ask him how he dreamed up his memorable yet often-mocked moniker: The Most Famous Artist. He says he just went to Google and typed in "Who is the most famous artist?" When he found that no one had yet claimed that title for themselves (or the web domain www.themostfamousartist.com), he did. He tells me that this idea, too, came out of his days in advertising; he chose his new name based on the SEO traffic it could drive. And now, if you Google "Who is the most famous artist?" along with Monet and Picasso you'll see results for Matt Monahan. So, as far as search engines are concerned, he just might be the most famous artist.

As Matt describes it, the idea for the brand of The Most Famous Artist came first; the art followed suit. His primary invention was the marketing strategy—the creative way in which he'd sell himself as an artist. The actual art pieces to be sold were the lesser inventions. In his search to find something he could successfully sell, he realized something many master amateurs discover when it's time to start over: *If I can sell anything—and I can sell anything—I might as well sell myself.*

In Matt's case, he sold a carefully crafted version of himself. He positioned himself as an "anti-artist"—a painter who can't paint and yet somehow paints for a living. To sell this image, he fully reversed the usual sequence of steps that gain people notoriety. Usually, people make something worthy of media coverage and wait for the media to cover it. Instead, Matt approached media outlets empty-handed, sold them a newsworthy headline, and if an outlet agreed to run the story, he'd make them the art to go with the story.

"Did you ever worry about being able to produce what you sold?" I ask him.

He shrugs. He'd be more worried to do it the other way, he says—to invest time, energy, and money in producing something without knowing if there's demand for it. That's just basic market research, he asserts. It's basic economics. Don't let the fact that it's also art fool you. Even in art, the way to make money is to find out what people want and then give them that.

൞ ൞ ൞

Matt had no cofounder or cocreator of The Most Famous Artist, but he did have a coconspirator. At the same moment he was laying the groundwork for TMFA, a new visual-first social network called Instagram was gaining traction. Matt saw Instagram as a great litmus test for whether people were (or could be) interested in his art. The art world didn't take him seriously, but if people liked his work on Instagram—literally and figuratively—he could sell it to them directly.

Once art agents, galleries, and dealers realized they were missing out on their cut of his sales, he figured they'd hop on board the TMFA train.

So, Matt's first goal as TMFA was simple (and now somewhat cliché): get tons of Instagram followers. Instead of learning the skills involved in making fine art, he learned what made for a popular Instagram account. He analyzed the types of shots that got attention and the cadence of posting that kept people interested. He studied the anatomy of Instagram accounts with the care and attentiveness Botticelli would employ when drawing his models.

From his research, he saw that people liked taking pictures of themselves, and people liked "liking" pictures of other people. This was a successful engagement loop among Instagram users. But there was a problem. The interiors of most people's homes proved drab, repetitive backdrops. Each person had only so many visually appealing backgrounds available to them.

In other words, the "selfie" phenomenon was happening, and with it an increasing demand for cool, photogenic places in which people could snap pictures of themselves.

TMFA was happy to fulfill this demand. He took to painting bright, simple murals all over LA's outdoor spaces for the express purpose of taking selfies. One of his murals—the super-meta #selfiewall in Venice Beach (a wall with the word *selfie* written over and over again in neat rows)—is by some accounts the most Instagrammed mural of all time.

Between his selfie murals and altered flea-market paintings, TMFA achieved popularity. Every time he'd post a new painting to Instagram, he'd receive at least a few messages from followers offering to buy it. He was also getting bolder and more conceptual. In early 2017, he approached Los Angeles city officials and asked if he could paint a few condemned houses in the Pico-Union neighborhood as an art installation. They agreed, and TMFA brazenly painted the entire city block—houses, sidewalks, trash cans, trees, hedges, and grass—Pepto-Bismol pink.

⚘ ⚘ ⚘

As I'm talking to him, I'm struck by how strategic (and frankly, cold) Matt makes this career reboot out to be. As he tells it, the invention of The Most Famous Artist and the art that followed were entirely calculated. He had no interest in art before realizing it could make him money.

"Don't you love art even a little?" I beseech him.

"No," he replies, "I actually don't like making art."

He assures me, despite my prolonged disbelief, that the making of art is not an activity he would do for fun. Most artists start out drawn to the activity of painting because they enjoy it. Most artists—even professional artists—begin in the tradition of the original amateur, the *amator*: "lover of."

Matt is not one of them. He makes art because it's a good financial investment and because The Most Famous Artist was the highest-margin product he could think of to sell. He understands that in a world where one's career can be ripped out from under them at any moment, good financial investments are good. He's not an amateur driven by love; he's a master amateur demonstrating financial durability.

Sensing my need for there to be some deeper component to this, Matt admits that he did want to be an artist, even if he never wanted to make art. "In Silicon Valley, you're in the tech circuit. In LA, you're in the entertainment circuit. In New York, you're in the financial circuit. I wanted to be an artist because I wanted to be in the art circuit—the culture circuit." He reflects for a moment. "Even when I was running an ad network, I didn't know what I was doing. So, I guess I'd rather be a fraud in the culture circuit than a fraud in the tech circuit."

This gives me pause, as it's practically the opposite of what Charu said motivated her. She wanted to make a film—she did not want to be a filmmaker. Matt wanted to be an artist—he did not want to make art. This makes me think there's an increasing disassociation between *work* and *work identity* that many master amateurs are using to their advantage. You no longer need to want both—the work and the identity, the activity and the title. To make a name for yourself, it seems to be sufficient to pursue one or the other.

༆ ༆ ༆

A few years into his career as an artist, TMFA started producing conceptual art designed to tackle his most favorite subject: greed. He produced an art-object series called *$100K*, in which he wrapped ten bricks of cash (each brick contained one thousand individual bills of legal US tender) in rubber bands and cellophane. He sold the bricks—charging $5,000 apiece—to eager buyers self-selected from his pool of 150,000 Instagram followers. All ten bricks were sold in less than twelve hours.

TMFA designed *$100K* to be a greedy man's dilemma. It's a kind of Schrödinger's cat for the avaricious. A buyer could, in theory, break open his brick of cash and potentially end up with more than the $5,000 he paid for it (TMFA assured buyers that some bricks had more than $5,000 cash in them, and all had at least $1,198). Or a buyer could hold on to his brick in hopes that TMFA's brand continues to gain popularity and then sell it at a later date for more than he paid.

Or the third option: don't be a greedy asshole, and just value art for art's sake.

To me, *$100K* is a very timely work of art because it lays bare the tension between *material* worth and *invented* worth. In the past, most products that people bought had material worth. A fine fur coat cost more than a cloth coat because it lasted longer and provided better protection against the elements. High-priced goods had easily comprehensible, corporeal benefits: warmth, safety, sanitation, and the like.

Today, we'll buy any number of esoteric products—products that have little or no material worth—because they have great invented worth. We'll pay a consultant for advice. We'll pay a life coach to act as a supportive sounding board. We'll buy a whole litany of objectively unnecessary "lifestyle" products to feel a certain way about ourselves. And as TMFA knows all too well, we'll buy a talentless artist's art because it seems cool.

These esoteric products—the products of our time—are being invented and championed all around us. By whom? Amateurs, of course. What will these products mean for the future of "making a living"? That's a question financially durable master amateurs will answer in due time.

As my conversation with Matt Monahan comes to a close, I ask him what kind of art he'll make next. He says that although he'll likely always make art, he's now interested in selling other types of products as well, specifically cryptocurrency and legal marijuana.

"If you think you'll make art for the rest of your life, would you ever consider going to art school?" I ask him, mostly on a hunch.

"Actually"—he chuckles—"I'm applying right now to a master-of-fine-arts program at Yale." He releases a big sigh. "I know . . . I'll probably leave disgusted, but I figured I should try."

A few months later, I decide on a whim to see what's for sale on TMFA's website. And right there, next to his signature "Go fucking do it then" T-shirt, is a new shirt with "FUCK YALE" scrawled across it. It seems, for the time being, the art establishment is still not ready to accept Matt Monahan as one of their own. Good for him, though, that he knows how to turn everything—even rejection—into profit.

FOR PROFIT

Successful master amateurs identify and invent innovative revenue streams all around them. They do not limit the scope of what they can sell to traditional goods and services. Instead, they see the potentiality for profit in everything they say, do, think, experience, and make.

To a master amateur, everything is, or at least can be, worth something, including one's skills, ideas, physical capacity, time—anything that can be claimed as one's own. This means anything and everything is a potential product to be sold.

This tendency to see dollar signs everywhere is *greed* in the traditional sense of the word, and it's also not. Master amateurs want to get paid, and generally speaking, the more they get paid, the better. They are unapologetically for profit and don't feel the same wariness about the "commodification of everything" that more vocationally conservative people feel. But at its core, this instinct to make money any way possible is a survival instinct. It's an adaptation to our new fiscal reality.

Despite the wealth our nation and world has accumulated, it's curiously hard to make a living these days. Most Americans work without pay in the form of school for a minimum of thirteen years, and if you earn a bachelor's degree after high school (which 40 percent of younger workers have), you're looking at more like seventeen years.[2] There's a decent chance you'll come out of higher education in debt and then be expected to work low-wage or contract jobs or invest in unpaid internships. Then there's the lifelong threat of job instability and the occasional dissolution of an entire industry.

Many people (especially people in their twenties and thirties, who on average earn 20 percent less than previous generations did at the same age) are disillusioned with the idea of one, solitary path toward making a living.[3] They see opportunity, expansiveness, and even freedom in the impending commodification of everything.

Of course, money does corrupt, and when one starts looking at everything as a product to be sold, there's the possibility of becoming immoral or manipulative. But, on the whole, *unorthodox commodification* is liberating people once confined to a professional path that takes decades (at least) to make a decent living. It offers limitless opportunities to make a living outside the handful of things we tend to believe we can make a living at. No one is capitalizing on these opportunities more than amateurs.

Much of this expansion of opportunities is owed to the internet and the advent of online platforms designed to sell goods, fund projects, and facilitate for-profit relationships. Matt Monahan used Instagram to sell his artwork, but there are a slew of sites designed to get you paid for whatever you have to offer.

There are peer-to-peer marketplaces like eBay, Etsy, and Depop, as well as crowdfunding platforms like GoFundMe, Kickstarter, and Patreon—the last of which beckons on its website, "Creators, come get paid."[4] There are freelancer sites like Upwork, which declares it's "creating a world of work without limits," and Fiverr, the freelancer site so in touch with nominal worth that its very name comes from their starting price per job: five dollars.[5]

With these platforms and many others like them, people are buying and selling the oddest things ever. On Fiverr, you can hire someone to break up with your significant other for you, cast a protection spell on you, or mail your enemies envelopes full of glitter.[6] Once, an eBay seller stated, "I have discovered the reason for our existence and will be happy to share this information with the highest bidder." Eight people were intrigued enough to bid, and "the meaning of life" sold for a measly (or exorbitant) $3.26.[7]

But don't be fooled—not all neo-goods are selling for chump change. In 2013, zany entrepreneur Jason Zook auctioned off his last name for $50,000. He also reportedly made $1 million in five years by wearing a different company's T-shirt every day.[8] Back in 2005, a web designer named Andrew Fischer auctioned off his forehead as advertising space. SnoreStop, an inconspicuous company selling snore remedies, bought the use of his forehead for one month for $37,375.[9]

It's easy to see these sales as oddities, silly expressions of internet debauchery—bizarre yet inconsequential exchanges. But some neo-goods and services are highly meaningful—even life changing—for those buying and selling.

For example, there's the relatively recent phenomenon of paying someone to help you have a child. Egg donors, surrogates, gestational carriers—these providers are not "selling their bodies" as some sort of gimmick. They're giving of themselves in a beautiful and meaningful way. Albeit, *not* for free. This, too, is inventive profit making. This, too, is a result of the "commodification of everything." These highly consequential products are the products of our time too.

※ ※ ※

The vast majority of us were raised to believe that one makes money from a career—a professional endeavor—and with rare exception, everything outside that profession should stay removed from profit making. One's own body, personal relationships, home, and family life should be kept sacred and as far away from profit making as possible. Wouldn't it be weird to pay a friend to listen to your woes? Wouldn't it feel wrong to charge a neighbor for an occasional plant watering? What kind of monstrous parent would you be if you ran up your child's bill for all the hours of childcare you've given them?

But in reality, we're moving in this direction. Many goods and services that were once exchanged pro bono within a home, family, or local community have become things people buy and sell through markets.[10] Just look at the commodification of one's home through sites like Airbnb. Another example—meal-delivery services—is now a $400 million industry and expected to grow tenfold in the next few years.[11] But a short few decades ago, no one would think of paying to have meals delivered every night. Meal prep was an activity squarely done for free among members of a family.

A number of jobs that we take for granted as being jobs are actually the for-profit versions of services people used to get for free from their community. These include day-care providers, financial advisors, party planners, and wedding officiates, to name a few.

From the ashes of traditional family and community responsibilities has come the for-profit job performed by strangers. Some may find this sad, but a master amateur sees in it an opportunity. There's the opportunity to make money, of course—as most "new" careers are first populated by inventive amateurs—and there's also the opportunity to form new kinds of social bonds.

To a master amateur, relationships based on the exchange of money are not inherently bad. Desire for money is not inherently bad. In fact, many master amateurs see money as one of the few things that consistently bring people together in these strange times. The more innovative opportunities we can create to earn and prosper together, the better.

But let's be real. Money *can* corrupt. There are dangers to monetizing your very existence—dangers to yourself and, even more so, to your consumers. When an amateur looks around and sees everything as a product to be sold, how can his customers know they're not being sold bad goods? When does greed in the hands of an amateur become a bad thing?

I think the only way to see the line between "good" greed and "bad" greed is to tell the stories of some bad amateurs—amateurs who've caused people physical and financial harm through dishonest profiteering. These are our cautionary tales; these are the people we don't want to be. These are the charlatans.

THE CHARLATANS

During America's roaring 1920s and depressed '30s, an amateur swindler named William J. A. Bailey manufactured and sold radioactive water as a cure-all to a public entranced by Marie Curie's discovery of radiation. Bailey held no medical degree but regularly referred to himself as Dr. Bailey. He had gone to Harvard as an undergrad but had dropped out after three semesters due to mounting debt. He'd later claim to be a Harvard graduate, as well as a doctor graduated from the University of Vienna and an expert in the therapeutic effects of low-level radiation.

Bailey spent his early adulthood launching questionable pharmaceutical businesses before creating Radithor, a health tonic that Bailey "asserted was the result of years of laboratory research, but which was really just distilled water laced with one microcurie each of two isotopes of radium."[12] Sold over the counter at pharmacies, Radithor was marketed to treat over 150 ailments, including the common cold, influenza, anemia, constipation, asthma, diabetes, mental illness, and erectile dysfunction.

Bailey personally guaranteed that Radithor was "harmless in every respect."[13]

It's hard to know what Bailey truly believed about his invention—whether he thought it was a legitimate medical treatment or an ineffectual yet harmless product from which he could profit . . . or if he knew it was a lethal substance and he decided to sell it anyway. What *is* known is that between 1925 and 1930, Bailey sold four hundred thousand bottles of Radithor at the steep price of one dollar per bottle (a newspaper at the time cost two cents), making Radithor a product with a profit margin of roughly 400 percent.[14]

One avid Radithor fan was millionaire steel tycoon Eben Byers, who, having injured himself on a "party train" following a Harvard-Yale football game, utilized Radithor to treat his chronic pain. He'd later testify to the Federal Trade Commission that he drank two to three bottles of Radithor a day and around fourteen hundred bottles in two years' time.

At first he felt exhilarated on Radithor, he testified. Then his teeth started falling out.

In 1932—just five years after his injury—Eben Byers died of brain cancer caused by radiation poisoning. He was so "hot" when he died that he had to be buried in a lead-lined coffin. Bailey was never prosecuted for Byers's death, but under the weight of federal investigation, he shut down his production of Radithor and moved on to making seaweed supplements. He forever disputed the claim than Byers's death was caused by Radithor, stating, "I have drunk more radium water than any man alive, and I have never suffered any ill effects."[15]

Bailey died seventeen years later of bladder cancer.

༄ ༄ ༄

On February 2, 2016, "Padre" Erwin Mena was arrested in Elysian Park, Los Angeles, at the age of fifty-nine. Upon his arrest, he was charged with twenty-two felonies and eight misdemeanors for the crimes of perjury, forgery, petty theft, grand theft, and most notably, impersonating a priest.

For close to two decades, Mena had performed masses and funeral services at various Southern California churches, took confessions, led prayer groups, and celebrated baptisms—just like any other Roman Catholic priest would. Except Mena was not an ordained priest. He was a fraudulent drifter who liked to show up at Catholic churches, wearing vestments and claiming to be their substitute priest, whenever a resident father was on vacation.

Mena was known to fill time between church services by selling parishioners the life story of Pope Francis on CD as well as a book he claimed to have written called *Confessions of a Renegade Catholic Priest*. Police later uncovered that the CDs were pirated, the book was plagiarized, and the money was pocketed.

Despite his salesy vibe, parishioners liked "Padre" Mena and looked forward to his sporadic visits. The congregation at Saint Ignatius of Loyola in Highland Park was particularly fond of Mena and invited him to stay as a visiting priest for five full months. When Mena announced he'd be organizing a group pilgrimage to see Pope Francis, congregants were thrilled.

Mena sold members of Saint Ignatius of Loyola, as well as members of other congregations, all-inclusive trips to see the pope for anywhere between $500 and $1,000 a pop. Ostensibly, the money was for airfare and humble accommodations in local convents. More than two dozen parishioners signed up, and Mena allegedly pocketed close to $53,000.

Whenever an expectant trip-goer would ask "Padre" for details, like trip dates or flight information, he'd benevolently remind them that patience is a virtue.

Mena got away with his impersonation for so long because, as LAPD detective Gary Guevara described it, "He looked like a priest, he walked like a priest, he could talk like a priest all the way to the very end." But on one particular feast day, Mena fumbled the Mass. "It was a complicated Mass that some of the real professional church ladies have memorized," Guevara said, "and literally the jig was all up." The "professional church ladies" reported Mena to the archdiocese, who in turn reported him to police.[16]

It's worth noting that the crime here is not leading a religious congregation. "A defrocked or retired priest could theoretically start up their own 'storefront church' with a ministry certificate from the Internet," the Catholic News Agency explained. "Mena's offense is specifically that he pretended to be a Roman Catholic, sacrament-distributing priest."[17]

In other words, it wasn't the saying of Mass that precipitated the fall of "Padre" Erwin Mena. It was profiteering through intentional misrepresentation.

༄ ༄ ༄

In 2011, Manhattan-based art gallery Knoedler & Company abruptly closed its doors amid a forgery scandal of epic proportions, in which the gallery was accused of pedaling $80 million worth of fraudulent paintings. Until the scandal rocked the once-prestigious gallery, Knoedler had the distinction of being the oldest art gallery in New York City.

Knoedler was brought down, in no small part, by a single elderly man painting out of a tiny apartment in Queens. Pei-Shen Qian had immigrated to the US from China in 1981 and, struggling to make a living given a significant language barrier, took to painting portraits of passersby on a Lower Manhattan street corner. It was on that street corner in the '90s that he was "discovered" by art dealers who allegedly saw in Qian's talent the making of a fraudulent painting enterprise.

José Carlos Bergantiños Díaz, his brother, and his former girlfriend Glafira Rosales—the dealers—frequented high-end galleries like Knoedler, claiming to represent an anonymous, wealthy client with a stash of rare inherited paintings. The trio passed off sixty-three of Qian's paintings as newly discovered pieces from masters of abstract expressionism like Mark Rothko, Jackson Pollock, and Willem de Kooning. Allegedly, Knoedler paid $20.7 million for Qian's forgeries and in return made $43 million in profit off their sales.

Qian has consistently denied knowledge of the scheme, claiming the dealers were solely responsible for the misrepresentation. He argued that the proof is in the paycheck. He was never paid more than $8,000 for any single "imitation" painting despite the multimillion-dollar prices they fetched at auction.

But according to the FBI's indictment, Qian repeatedly and knowingly forged the signatures of famous painters on his creations. And there's evidence he aged the paintings by using old canvases and paint, staining them with tea bags, heating them with a hair dryer, and leaving them exposed to wind and snow. In a sworn statement, US Attorney Preet Bharara called Qian and the dealers "modern masters of forgery and deceit," adding that the case "paint[s] a picture of perpetual lies and greed."[18]

Why are William J. A. Bailey, "Padre" Erwin Mena, and Pei-Shen Qian charlatans and not master amateurs? Because they misrepresented themselves and what they were selling. They intentionally deceived others for personal gain and, in the process, discredited anything valuable they may have had to offer. They were amateurs in addition to being charlatans, but—as these important distinctions go—the crime in these cases was not being an amateur. The crime was being dishonest.

It's not a crime to manufacture health supplements, but it is a crime to falsely claim to be a medical doctor. Leading a religious congregation is not a crime; lying about being an ordained priest is. Painting in the style of a famous artist is not a crime as long as you're honest about what you're doing. When you're a master amateur, you can *do* whatever you want. As long as you're truthful about who you are.

HONESTY! THE NEW CURE-ALL

Great master amateurs aren't shy about desiring money, maximizing their earning potential, and seeking out high-margin products to sell. They do not equate *selling* with *selling out*. They think the ability to conjure saleable goods out of nothing and everything will be a critical skill in an increasingly unstable job market.

However, master amateurs don't misrepresent themselves or what they're selling in their pursuit of profits. If you misrepresent yourself, omit vital information, mislead, or outright lie to consumers, you're embodying some of the worst amateur stereotypes. You probably *are* a swindler, a charlatan, or a harmful fraud.

Now, one more point on this. We all know that lying for profit can hurt others. But lying for profit can also hurt *you*. Even if you're totally self-interested, you still shouldn't lie, because lying will derail you from ever becoming a master of amateurism. You can't discredit yourself and last long enough in amateurism to become a master.

In amateurism, being honest is not just the right thing to do; it's also a self-serving, self-preservational act. You're already an amateur—give yourself the commercial advantage of at least being a trustworthy one.

In other words, transparency is a path to longevity (and increased earning potential in the long run) as an amateur. Transparency is the thing that makes Matt Monahan's art work. So, if you're a painter who can't paint, admit it. If you're "fake as fuck," just say that. Some people—your potential customers—will appreciate it. And if nobody's buying what you're selling in earnest, improve your product. Go back to chapter 2, and call what you've got an amendment-ready first try.

Consumers do have a responsibility to vet the products and services they buy—especially the esoteric neo-products that now flood the market. But consumers can't successfully vet anything if you lie to them. I'm no moral philosopher (not yet, anyway), but morality as a master amateur doesn't seem all that complicated to me. Make money wherever you can, and don't be a charlatan.

CHAPTER 4
PERSONAL RESPONSIBILITY

The time is always right to do what is right.
—Dr. Martin Luther King Jr.

THE CALL TO AMATEURISM

As Sheila Wysocki describes it, she was half-asleep when she decided to become a private investigator. The day it happened, her house in suburban Tennessee was uncharacteristically quiet with her husband at work, her boys at school, and her typically clamorous dogs subdued by God knows what.

Sheila, entrenched in assigned reading for a Bible-study course, decided to move her homework session from the desk to the bed. She'd struggled with dyslexia since childhood, and now, at age forty-two, reading really took it out of her. So, before getting too deep into the visions of the prophet Daniel, she lay down and closed her eyes for just a second.

Then, standing at the foot of her bed was Angie.

Sheila rose from her half sleep and stared at the vision—at Angie, dressed in the outfit she'd worn the day they first met—from behind her Xylonite plastic reading glasses. The bed pillow had matted down Sheila's chocolate-brown pageboy haircut, and before she could even zhush it back up, the vision was gone.

Sheila took a sharp breath. She set her Bible aside and picked up the landline beside the bed. She planted her feet in the carpet and dialed the phone number for the Dallas Police Department—a number she'd never forgotten.

It's time, she thought. The words rang like a bell in her mind. *Okay, Angie. It's time now.*

༄ ༄ ༄

On October 12, 1984, Angie Samota was murdered in a condominium located just blocks from the Southern Methodist University campus in Dallas, Texas. She was twenty years old, a sophomore at SMU, and one of the few female computer-science and electrical-engineering majors in the country.

Angie had cherubic features and a personality to match. She styled her long auburn hair in big, bouncy Texas curls. Her eyes were a buoyant, unsaturated blue. In the last moments of her life, she was raped and then stabbed eighteen times in the chest with a kitchen knife likely plucked from her own condo. The scene was so savage, police originally thought the killer had tried to carve her heart out.

Angie's good friend and former roommate, Sheila Wysocki (née Gibbons), was visiting her parents in northern Texas the night Angie was murdered. The two had been randomly paired as roommates their freshman year and had grown to be great friends, living together until Sheila moved into her sorority house her sophomore year. It was one of those sorority sisters who called Sheila up at her parents' house to tell her Angie hadn't shown up to the big SMU versus Baylor football game, because she was dead.

In those first days after the murder, Sheila actively helped the police identify people in Angie's world. There was no forced entry into the condo, and the crime occurred late at night, so both Sheila and the police believed the killer was someone Angie knew. At the top of the list were Angie's boyfriend, her former boyfriend, and a male friend with whom she'd danced at a club the night she was murdered. However, police quickly determined the men's alibis all checked out and no physical evidence could tie any of them to the scene. After six months of investigation, to Sheila's chagrin, the case went cold.

Once it went cold, Sheila says, the devastation left her unable to function—unable to finish college even if she'd wanted to. "When Angie was murdered, I left school," Sheila would later tell me. "I walked off campus and never turned around." In another interview, she remembered her break with higher education this way: "I always think that I wasn't meant to go to college. The only reason I think I went to college was to meet Angie."[1]

College had educated Sheila, but not in the way anyone expected. It had taught her that bad (no, atrocious) things can happen to good (no, wonderful) people. It also taught her that it's the choice of decent people to do or not do something about that.

℘ ℘ ℘

In lieu of getting a college degree, Sheila got married, had two sons, and started a series of successful retail businesses, including the first rent-a-dress business for wedding and formal wear in Dallas. By 2004—the year she saw Angie at the foot of her bed—Sheila considered herself an occasional businesswoman and a full-time, loud-and-proud stay-at-home mom.

Compelled by her vision (or memory, or ghost, or God knows what), Sheila suddenly felt the need to speak to Virgil Sparks, the homicide detective assigned to Angie's case back in the '80s. He'd surely listen to the answering-machine message she'd left, remember her, and call her right back. She'd invited him to her wedding back in the '80s, after all.

He did not call her right back. Forty-eight hours later, Sheila called him again. Now, one thing to know about Sheila Wysocki: she's persistent. She does not take no (or silence, for that matter) for an answer. "If I want to talk to you," she tells me, "I will call, text, email, hunt you down, find your mom, your sister, your brother . . . I wanna talk to you!"

Sheila called DPD again and again, leaving message after message. Again and again—ring, ring, ring—nothing. She'd later tell the producers of NBC's *Dateline* that she left DPD at least fifty answering-machine messages before someone deigned to call her back. When she finally did connect with a detective, he told her that no one had called about Angie's case in twenty years. Sheila hung up the phone, cried, and a few hours later called again.

This time, she had a specific question in mind. Since she'd been involved in the investigation of Angie's murder in those early days, she knew for a fact that semen, blood, and fingernails were collected from the crime scene. She also knew (from watching the O. J. Simpson trial in the '90s) that DNA could help identify killers. She suddenly needed to know: Had that evidence ever been tested for DNA?

At first, DPD told her that the evidence of which she spoke had been lost in a flood. Unconvinced, Sheila just kept asking about it. "I cannot tell you how many times I heard that they did not have the evidence. And something told me . . . that's not true."[2] She called hundreds of times—by her estimate, seven hundred times over the course of a couple of years—to insist that someone from the department find the lost evidence and reopen the case.

Eventually, Sheila's telephonic water torture worked.

Once—just once—a rookie detective answered Sheila's call and casually remarked that the Angie Samota case evidence was not lost. He could get it for her. Then the rookie paused and stuttered, "I'll ask my sergeant and call you right back." True to form, he never did. But it was enough. It was a meaty-enough bone to turn this suburban stay-at-home mom into a dogged, amateur sleuthhound.

Sheila digresses from the story of getting Angie's murder solved to explain something important. When you're close to a violent crime like that, she says, security becomes a necessity on par with food and water. Violence is never again something that's "out there"; it's something that can manifest no matter how mundane your surroundings seem.

For this reason, Sheila and her family lived in a gated community. She chatted frequently with her community's security guards about Angie's case and the DPD's lack of interest in solving it. One day, one of the guards suggested she get a private investigator's license. PIs get special privileges when it comes to accessing police evidence, he explained, and maybe—just maybe—DPD would test Angie's evidence for DNA if a PI was asking.

Sheila, spontaneously propelled by this long shot, threw herself into investigative fieldwork. She first convinced professional PIs to let her shadow them, and by observing them, she learned the fundamentals of surveillance. She then learned to shoot a gun, earned a concealed-weapons license, and—most challenging for her—she studied her heart out. In the moments when reading overwhelmed her, she got her teenage son to read criminal-justice textbooks to her out loud.

Since Sheila did not have any background in criminal justice or law enforcement, she took to attending any relevant class that would have her. It was a habit that stuck. "I've probably taken more classes than anybody with a criminal-justice degree. I still go to a class or conference about once a month. Every time I'm in a room with other PIs, I want to be the dumbest PI in there. I want to learn from everybody." She pauses. "There's probably an insecurity deep down that I don't have my degree, but I guess I use that insecurity to my advantage."

Within a year, Sheila had passed her state's PI licensing exam. Later, in 2011, she'd form her very successful PI firm: Without Warning Private Investigation. A fitting name, I think, considering her detective career came quite literally out of nowhere.

I ask Sheila if she had always had a latent interest in criminal investigation—an interest that was somehow awakened by that vision of Angie. "Not at all!" She laughs. If anything, she was someone who avoided thinking about violence at all costs. "This is not, in any form or fashion, a career I would have chosen. I still can't believe I'm doing it." She chuckles. "I simply felt compelled to learn enough to move Angie's case along. Angie's death was more important than anything to me."

I ask her if anyone—possibly her husband or sons—tried to talk her out of it. "Nobody tried to talk me out of it. Did they think it was the most ridiculous thing in the world that I was going to do it? Yes. It's actually hilarious to think I'm a PI. But just because you don't have the background doesn't mean you can't go out and learn it."

As it turned out, Sheila becoming a licensed PI *did* influence the Dallas Police Department to act on Angie's case. They never handed any evidence over to her, but as Sheila recalls in her unabashed way, "Me becoming a PI showed them I was never, *ever* going away." And one day, a detective phoned Sheila to inform her that DPD had formed a cold-case unit, Angie's case was at the top of the list, and the not-at-all-lost evidence had already been sent for DNA testing.

Two years later, DPD got a DNA hit on serial rapist Donald Andrew Bess, who was already serving a life sentence in a Texas correctional unit. Sheila had never even heard Bess's name before he was identified as Angie's killer. On June 18, 2010, he was convicted of Angie's murder and moved to Texas's death row. Angie's was the only cold case solved in the city of Dallas that entire year.

℘ ℘ ℘

In a world where wanting is a preeminent motivator for most people—wanting to *do* something, wanting to *be* something, wanting to *have* something—it's rare to meet someone for whom wanting played no part in a critical career decision. Charu Sharma wanted to make a film, Matt Monahan wanted to be an artist, but Sheila Wysocki wanted nothing whatsoever to do with investigating crimes. And yet she spun up a new career in her forties, with no relevant background, to do just that.

Why would someone make such a decision? I ask her.

"It wasn't really a decision," she says. "I was just called up."

"Called up . . ." I trail off.

"By God," Sheila confirms. "I have a name for it. I call it a 'God nod.' It's a moment when God gives you a nod on what you're supposed to do next." She thinks for a moment. "But I'm the type that needs the burning bush—I can't take subtle hints."

"Do you think that's why you were sent a full-blown vision?"

"I can't explain it. I just think that my life has been ruled by God nods."

"Was a 'God nod' responsible for you continuing your PI work after Angie's case was solved?"

"Actually, no!" she realizes. "I fully intended to retire my license. The only case I cared about was Angie's. I didn't really care about *crime*; I only cared about *my* crime."

But after Angie's case was solved and the press picked up on Sheila's role in making it happen, people started contacting her. She got one letter in the mail, then two letters, then five hundred letters. One thousand letters later, Sheila realized she couldn't rest knowing so many people were suffering. She tells me many of the letters were from women much like herself—women who wanted to know the status of a loved one's case and were being incessantly ignored by the system.

"When I read a letter," she says, "I can feel the person's pain. I know that they're not being heard. What I do is I *hear* these people."

Thirteen years into her criminal-investigation career, people still underestimate Sheila Wysocki. "When I go to court, I still have judges in the South act like I'm a housewife who does this for a hobby. I just came back from a conference of probably four hundred PIs, and there's always this moment when we go around and say what our backgrounds are. When it comes to me, I always say, 'Oh, I'm a mom.' The entire place goes quiet when I say that."

"How does that make you feel?"

"I think it's hilarious! I love proving people wrong. I love proving the judges wrong. I love proving district attorneys wrong. I love proving that you gotta start listening to regular people."

Sheila Wysocki has solved fifty-three cold cases in her career, including murders, missing-persons cases, and rape cases—with many more still being investigated. She does it because it's the right thing to do, and because, in her summation, God called her up for duty. She does it because someone has to do it, and a college dropout turned tenacious stay-at-home mom is as good for the job as any.

IF YOU WANT SOMETHING DONE RIGHT, YOU HAVE TO DIY

A great master amateur takes on any responsibility that he senses is his, even if doing so is not straightforwardly beneficial or appealing to him. When the compulsion strikes to take on an unsavory, unpleasant, or scary task, a great master amateur will step out on that limb if the impulse to do so just won't go away.

Master amateurs are not the only people who get these impulses—these sudden urges to help others, to speak out, to do what's right. Most everyone who's invested in the world has felt, at one point or another, the itch, the sting, the burning rash known as "something needs to be done about that."

A great number of people—professionals included—act on these impulses in altruistic ways. But when an amateur acts on a moral impulse, he tends to go bigger with it. He's more likely to drop everything and reinvent himself as the champion of a cause, not because he's a better person than a professional but because if anybody is going to give up everything to devote himself to a cause, wouldn't it be the person whose expertise is starting over?

In addition, amateurs tend to act on these impulses in grandiose ways because they've learned to take their impulses seriously. They're not going to repress an impulse to act because it's not straightforwardly sensible. If it's there, it's worth considering. They're also less dissuaded from acting on an impulse because of a lack of preexisting knowledge; they know they can learn what they need to know if they need to learn it.

Most importantly, unlike professionals, master amateurs are not in the business of maintaining a linear career trajectory, so deviating from their current work to follow a moral pursuit seems within reason. They don't have a coherent career story to lose, so they're freer than professionals are to pivot. One might say that pivoting *is* their career story.

So, master amateurs tend to get really righteous when the mood strikes them. While you might think I'm saying they're more selfless or self-effacing than professionals, I actually think it's the opposite. I think dutiful master amateurs are propelled by a productive version of self-centeredness: a propensity to see the world through the lens of the self, to relate the world's problems to the self, and to believe that they themselves are viable agents for change.

This worldview extends far beyond master amateurs. More and more, people are raised to see themselves as the center of the universe—everything is seen as somehow relating to oneself—and this rampant self-centeredness is a coin with two sides. The downside is entitlement, narcissism, and the hoarding of resources. The upside is a sense of personal responsibility that extends far beyond the traditional boundaries of one's family, community, or town.

In other words, the more each one of us thinks we're the center of the world, the more each one of us is inclined to feel personally responsible for the state of the world.

This grandiose sense of self-importance can cause people mental strife, to be sure—it can make you feel like you're not doing enough, not contributing enough, not having a big enough impact. But it can also translate into a surprising willingness (even eagerness) to take ownership of challenges that, in the past, would have been the exclusive burden of the authorities. When a problem got big enough, it became *their* problem, not *mine*.

Today, through disillusionment with authorities, self-empowerment, or both, this is no longer the typical mindset. Individuals now feel powerful and important enough to tackle issues of enormous scale on their own. They feel capable enough to become an amateur in order to make a difference.

℘ ℘ ℘

While we'll never reach consensus on a single definition of an *amateur*, we can all agree that no one is more amateurish than a high school kid. The occasional child prodigy aside, teenagers are the essence of amateurism. They have not lived enough years to fulfill the requirements of most professions, and the public-school curriculum forces them to be generalists before they can ever become specialists.

Nevertheless, a surprising number of teenagers are tackling the critical problems of our day—issues that a few decades ago people their age would not have had the audacity to touch—simply because they feel they must.

The social issue that's top of mind for many teens (because it's literally battering down their door) is gun violence. A flash point in the history of American gun violence came on March 18, 2018, when correspondents for *60 Minutes* interviewed five survivors of the shooting at Marjory Stoneman Douglas High School in Parkland, Florida. In the interview, one of the survivors, Cameron Kasky (aged seventeen), dubbed himself and his peers "the mass shooting generation."

The thirty-two students enrolled in American government class at LA's Alhambra High School watched that interview, and with the encouragement of their teacher, Mr. Sanchez, drafted their own gun-reform proposal. It outlined the changes to gun laws they believed this country needed: a ban on sales of military-grade weapons, no more online gun sales or gun-show loopholes, an extension of the minimum age to purchase a gun from eighteen to twenty-five, and a requirement that all purchasers attend a fourteen-day gun-training program.³

It's safe to say these kids were not experts in gun laws before the impulse to learn—to act—struck. But they successfully drafted what most experts would consider a reasonable gun referendum. And they didn't stop there. They presented their proposal to their city's Democratic Club, which agreed by unanimous vote to submit and endorse it to the LA County Democratic Party. In 2019, Representative Judy Chu presented the kids' referendum before Congress.

The closing line of the referendum laid out the students' intentions in no uncertain terms: "BE IT FURTHER RESOLVED, we the students of Mr. Sanchez's third period American government class have taken it upon ourselves to bring about the change that we would like to see."⁴

Another issue that's weighing heavily on the minds of young people is climate change. In February 2018, thirteen kids (ranging in ages from seven to seventeen) filed a lawsuit against the state of Washington, claiming lawmakers' refusal to pass aggressive carbon-emission limitations was infringing upon their generation's civil rights.⁵ In Utah, students attending Logan High School successfully convinced their Republican governor to sign a resolution acknowledging the reality of climate change. The kids first submitted such a resolution in 2017, but it was rejected. They spent the next two years talking to policy makers and revising it until it convinced even the adults in power to take action.⁶

Pick any pressing social problem of our day, and there's probably a young person working on it. At eight years old, Hannah Taylor founded a charity to help homeless people in Canada. The charity has currently raised over $3 million.⁷ While still in high school, Tess Flemma started a nonprofit to distribute aquaponics systems (sustainable, soil-free farming units) to Peruvian locals to combat deforestation in the

Amazon. Flemma once said, "I wake up knowing that I want to help the rain forest, and after seeing the devastation am happy to know I am at least contributing a small part towards saving it."[8]

In 2017, three seventh-grade girls from Oregon learned about the impending end of net neutrality from an Instagram post. Outraged, they summoned the courage to testify before the Oregon House Committee on Rules in favor of a bill that would make it illegal for government to work with internet service providers that throttle internet access for profit. The bill passed, thanks in small part to those three seventh-grade girls. One of them, then twelve years old, closed her testimony to Congress with the kind of blistering statement only a child can make: "When kids get involved, you know someone really screwed up."[9]

There's a seed of belief buried deep in these young people—one that goes something like this: *When the world is heading in the wrong direction, it needs me to help set it right. At least, I could help set it right, so why not try?*

Call this empowerment, entitlement, social consciousness, or the "me" generation to the nth degree. I think it's simply the spirit of amateurism—the understanding that it's good to try even when you don't know what's going to happen. It's a philosophy beloved of dutiful master amateurs young and old, that if you want something done right—something big, small, or critical on a cosmic scale—you have to do it yourself.

MEETING THE NEED

Clara Barton was thirty-nine years old when the Civil War made a stop at her doorstep. Untraditional, unmarried, and already on her second career, Clara worked at the US Patent Office in Washington, DC, when the war began in 1861. She had, just a few years earlier, left her first career as a schoolteacher in Massachusetts to become the country's first female patent clerk.

She would later—much later—become America's first female diplomat, the first woman honored with a US historical site, and the first woman to establish a disaster-relief organization: the American Red Cross.

But back in April 1861, Clara was mired in a war with her boss, Secretary of the Interior Robert McClelland, who had demoted her to copyist in an attempt to drive her out of the patent office. He did not believe women should work in government. Clara, sick and weary of fighting, went to the train station to divert her mind. She'd heard that wounded Union soldiers would be entering the city any day now. She thought perhaps she could lend a hand.

When Clara arrived, she saw soldiers piled up at the train station; local hospitals were woefully underprepared to care for them all. She got closer and recognized one of the men, then another, and then another. She was shocked; she recognized many of these men. These were "her boys"—boys she'd grown up with in Oxford, Massachusetts. Some had even been her pupils back when she was a schoolteacher.

Clara, spontaneously propelled by these familiar, bloodied faces, sprang into action. She rallied round the boys from the Sixth Massachusetts Regiment—"her boys"—and instructed them to go set up camp in the Senate. When the First Rhode Island Regiment arrived, she sent them to the patent office to rest. She set herself the task of gathering supplies—entreating acquaintances to donate any food, clothes, or provisions they could.

By the time she'd amassed three warehouses of supplies, Clara had made the decision not to hand them over to the authorities. No one would distribute these supplies other than herself. Her second career having been fully derailed by the sight of "her boys," Clara left the patent office at the end of 1861 and launched a third career as an intrepid amateur army nurse.

༄ ༄ ༄

Today, Clara Barton is remembered as a treasured symbol of American volunteerism, but in those early days as an independent nurse, she was viewed with great suspicion. She had never been to nursing school (nursing was predominantly a male profession at the time), and she had no formal medical training. Moreover, women who followed troops around were highly scrutinized. They were usually performing a different type of job.

And Clara, by her own admission, did not possess a personality that engendered confidence. She was stubborn and yet painfully shy—a condition that "increased rather than diminished over time." In her autobiography, *The Story of My Childhood*, she described herself as "diffident, timid, non-committal, afraid of giving trouble, and difficult to understand."[10]

Nevertheless, Clara became inexplicably brave in battle. She'd approach the front lines to administer aid, tending to injured soldiers with wild disregard for her own safety. Legend has it that one time she got so close to active fighting, a bullet shot straight through her coat sleeve and killed the soldier to whom she was tending.

But Clara did not get a free pass to hero status because of her bravery. The late 1800s was a time of increasing professionalization in the US, and medical professionals were actively trying to get volunteers (however noble their intentions) off the fields and out of the hospitals. Clara's biographer, Elizabeth Brown Pryor, described the very presence of volunteers at that time as "anathema to those who were trying so hard to establish themselves as skilled professionals in the medical field."[11]

For this reason, Clara frequently "ran into conflict with professional zealots who wanted to eliminate charitable work done by any who did not have academic training and scientific motivation."[12]

The professional zealots held up Clara's aid efforts for over a year. It wasn't until the Battle of Cedar Mountain in August 1862 that she finally obtained all the permissions required to distribute her supplies. She then, according to the doctor on duty, "appeared at a field hospital at midnight with a wagon-load of supplies drawn by a four-mule team."[13] He would later say of her, "I thought that night if heaven ever sent out a[n] ... angel, she must be one—her assistance was so timely."[14]

Clara was from then on known as the Angel of the Battlefield. She would go on to aid soldiers at every major Civil War battle fought in Maryland, Virginia, and South Carolina.

Clara Barton was not fond of talking about her reasons for taking on such dangerous and difficult work. We can be led to believe, though, that she did not have much to say about her reasons, because they were not her focus. She didn't do this work to satisfy a personal ambition. She did it because it needed to be done.

"You must never so much as think whether you like [the work] or not, whether it is bearable or not," she once said. "You must never think of anything except the need, and how to meet it."[15]

THE SELF AND THE RIGHT

While we're not in the throes of a civil war at this moment in history, there are plenty of pressing issues to be addressed these days—some arguably bigger than the fate of any given nation.

Master amateurs like Sheila Wysocki, Clara Barton, and the students of Mr. Sanchez's third-period American government class demonstrate a rambunctious do-it-yourself energy that's just right for tackling the important issues of our day.

It's an energy that emerges when everyone—even laypeople—can see that *something needs to be done about that*. It's an energy that often irritates those in charge—just ask the Dallas Police Department or the medical professionals of 1861. It's the spirit of individual contribution come to life, an empowered amateur energy that has the potential to push nonsense aside and allow the decent thing to emerge.

This empowered amateur energy can spring up spontaneously—as with Sheila and her vision, Clara and "her boys"—but I think it can also be generated intentionally. To generate it, one must simply apply oneself to what's right. Look at a need; then look at yourself and find the overlap.

This is one of the skills that amateurs practice as they master their craft. It's a core competency of a master amateur. It is, quite literally, the cultivation of self-righteousness: the application of the self to the right. In my opinion, *self-righteousness* is a word that's due for rehabilitation, just like *self-centered*, *arrogant*, and of course, *amateur*.

The world needs more self-centered people who see themselves as perfectly capable agents for change, regardless of the subject matter. The world needs more people arrogant enough to look at an intractable social problem—a problem with which even professionals struggle—and think, *I bet I could figure that out*.

These dutiful master amateurs know that they have little power over the evils of this world—war, crime, violence, and the rest—but they do have power over themselves. *I have myself,* they think. *So, I'll start there.* This self-centeredness is good; it makes them capable. It leads them to see a problem that someone must fix and think, *Well, why not me?*

CHAPTER 5

FREEDOM

I never said, "I want to be alone." I only said, "I want to be let alone!" There is all the difference.
—Greta Garbo

THE LONE RANGER

Forrest Mims III looks like a good guy out of an old western. In his official headshot, he's wearing a white cowboy hat—not gleaming white and not gray but the color of bone—and a denim button-up of the same color. His clean shave reveals weathered skin. On what looks to be a ranch, he sits upright, wrists on knees, with a look in his eye. He's lookin' at you like he thinks you're funny. His face is fashioned in a half-cocked smile.

At seventy-four years old, Forrest Mims is one of the great amateur scientists and technologists of our time. He's often credited as the most widely read amateur technologist of the computer age thanks to a series of thirty-six popular electronics guidebooks he authored for RadioShack in the '70s,

'80s, and '90s. The bestseller of the series, *Getting Started in Electronics*, has sold 1.3 million copies since its publication in 1983. The series as a whole sold over seven million copies and inspired a generation of technically minded kids to go build things for themselves.

In addition to his RadioShack books, Forrest has spent the last twenty-eight years recording changes in Earth's atmosphere. He monitors the ozone layer, water-vapor layer, radiation levels, and other parameters critical to understanding the state of our planet's climate. He does this independently, separate from any institution, using a handheld device he built himself. In 1993, he won a prestigious Rolex Award for Enterprise for the invention of his personal atmospheric-monitoring device. The award committee praised him—as institutions so rarely do—for possessing "a rare breadth of scientific and technical expertise in an age of narrow professionalism."[1]

Forrest has no formal education in science or technology. Despite this, he's published more than twenty papers in peer-reviewed journals, including *Nature* and *Science*, often with professional scientists as coauthors. He's consulted on numerous projects for the National Geographic Society and NASA's Goddard Space Flight Center, including a seminal survey of atmospheric changes in the Amazon rain forest.[2]

If you're not impressed yet, here's one more thing. When Forrest was twenty-five years old, he cofounded a technology company called MITS (Micro Instrumentation and Telemetry Systems), which built the first commercially successful personal computer.[3] Called the Altair 8800, MITS's build-it-yourself computer kit flew off the shelves after *Popular Electronics* magazine ran a feature on it in 1975. According to the Smithsonian Institution, the Altair was the "machine that inaugurated the personal computer age."[4] Early fans of the machine included Bill Gates and Paul Allen, the future founders of Microsoft.

Forrest, unlike some of the people I profile in this book, fully embraces his amateurism; he takes his amateurism seriously. In science, the line between amateur and professional is drawn in the sand, and Forrest knows which side he's on. "I get called a professional scientist sometimes," he tells me with his trademark matter-of-factness, "but I'm not."

"I also get called a citizen scientist," he continues, "but I have a bit of a problem with that idea. We know what 'amateur scientist' means. It means you do real science. You get published and you even work with professional scientists. Unfortunately, the typical citizen scientist is little more than a data collector for the professionals. Collecting data is not being a scientist." He chuckles. "If you want to be a scientist, be an amateur scientist."

༄ ༄ ༄

Forrest Mims III was born in Houston, Texas, in 1944. His father was a US Air Force pilot as well as an amateur artist and architect. Like many military kids, Forrest learned to be self-reliant at an early age. He started teaching himself science with gusto at age eleven, learning the basics of electronics from *National Geographic* magazine. His father encouraged Forrest's interests. Occasionally, his father would buy a model rocket or a crystal radio, each of which Forrest would take apart, modify, and rebuild—better.

Forrest's life of amateurism began when he was a kid visiting his great-grandpa in Lufkin, Texas. His great-grandpa was completely blind (he'd been blinded in a DuPont powder-keg explosion decades before), and yet he could navigate the streets of Lufkin as well as anyone in the family. One day, Forrest realized he did it by tapping utility poles with his cane as he walked.

"I looked up and said, 'How do you do that, Grampa?'" Forrest recalls. "He tried to explain, but he really couldn't. Finally he said, 'It's just something you learn how to do when you're blind.' Years later when he passed, I was in college and I just became highly motivated to do something to help blind people."

At twenty years old, Forrest set out to make a travel aid to the blind—a wearable device that'd help a blind person navigate his or her surroundings. To create it, Forrest analyzed electronic devices already in common use. The electromagnetic audio speaker (the kind that can play music and also record it) made sense to him as a model. The speaker worked as both an emitter and a receiver, meaning it produced audio waves and also detected them. If a similar device emitted light waves, Forrest thought, and detected the light that reflected off surrounding objects, a blind person could navigate around those objects.

Forrest had, through independent research, stumbled upon the principle that underpins radar technology. But to build a device that acted as one's own personal radar, Forrest needed the right kind of light-emitting diode. Only one company produced commercially available infrared light-emitting diodes—the perfect diodes. That company was Texas Instruments.

So, Forrest being Forrest, he walked off his college campus at Texas A&M University, stuck out his thumb, and hitchhiked up to Texas Instruments. Once there, he haggled his way into a conversation with a senior physicist, explained his idea, and asked for a diode. "[The physicist] said to me, 'They're very costly, but if you can build a circuit that works . . . I will send you one.'"

Forrest hitchhiked home and spent the next weekend building the circuit. He sent it up to Texas Instruments and, a few weeks later, received three infrared light-emitting diodes in the mail. "*Three* diodes," Forrest remembers with jubilation. "Can you believe? One thousand dollars' worth of diodes!"

I interrupt Forrest's recollections at this point to clarify one thing. "But, Forrest," I say, "you didn't major in electronics in college, right?"

"I did not," he confirms.

"Why not? You were obviously passionate about technology."

"Actually," he says, "the dean of research at Texas A&M asked me the same thing. He heard about the work I was doing and said, 'Why in the world didn't you major in electronics?'... The truth was, I just could not do math. My freshman algebra average was a D minus."

But, Forrest remembers, he figured he should at least check out the electrical engineering building. Maybe the students were doing great stuff over there. So Forrest—three years into his college career—walked over to the Electrical Engineering Building and eavesdropped on a class.

"There was a classroom full of guys," he recalls, "and they were seated at these benches. On the blackboards behind them there were all these math equations, and there was just no way I could understand any of them. But the thing is, these guys... they were building vacuum tubes."

Forrest pauses to let it sink in just how lame that is. As a nonengineer, I don't fully appreciate how lame vacuum tubes are. But I've come to understand that this would be like eavesdropping on a professional culinary school and seeing the advanced students boiling eggs.

"I was back in my dorm room building transistor circuits," he resumes. "I was sending my voice over a beam of light half a mile down a country road. I was building light sensors that could detect a match in the dark three hundred feet away!" Forrest guffaws. "And these guys were building vacuum tubes.

In that moment I decided 'I don't need to study electronics... I'd just... I'd just be building vacuum tubes!'"

※ ※ ※

Forrest graduated from Texas A&M University in 1966 with a degree in government and minors in English and history. The next year, he went to Vietnam as an intelligence officer and was stationed at the Tan Son Nhut Air Base just outside Saigon.

With him, he took prototypes of his travel aid to the blind, which he tested on pupils at the Saigon School for Blind Boys and Girls. He also took a stockpile of homemade model rockets, which he roguishly launched all over the air-force base. Once, his rocket launch triggered an army threat alert, and a helicopter gunship came to neutralize the threat. "I seriously thought I was going to get shot." Forrest giggles. It was only then he started notifying authorities before launching rockets in a war zone.

Not long into his military career, Forrest gained media attention for his travel aid to the blind. A story that ran in US newspapers caught the attention of one Colonel Jones of the Air Force Weapons Lab. Impressed, Jones insisted that Forrest come work at the weapons lab as soon as his tour in Vietnam ended.

Forrest was happy to oblige. "The problem was," he explains, "I had a liberal-arts degree, and to work at the weapons lab you needed either a master's or PhD in one of the sciences. The computer kept spitting my name out, and Colonel Jones kept going back and saying, 'No, I need him at the weapons lab.'"

Eventually, Colonel Jones overrode the system and secured Forrest a job at the lab, working on top-secret military tech. "If I told you what I worked on, I'd go to jail!" He laughs. "But I can tell you that I worked with very high-powered lasers and I learned so much about science. The weapons lab really taught me what I know about electronics."

While working at the weapons lab, Forrest became something of a star in the model-rocket world. In 1969, the editor of *Model Rocketry* magazine asked Forrest to write an article about the light-flashing recovery system he used in his rockets. Forrest obliged and was thrilled to receive $93.50 in the mail as payment. At that moment, he decided to leave the air force to become a freelance writer.

Over the next five years, Forrest would write articles for hobbyist magazines like *Model Rocketry* and *Popular Electronics*. He would found the company that would become MITS—the makers of the legendary Altair 8800—with his "rocket buddy" Ed Roberts. He'd also secure the book deal with RadioShack that'd lead to his immense influence on the next generation of engineers.

To those who grew up on his RadioShack books, Forrest has become something of a hometown hero. His books enlightened, but more than that, they empowered. They made curious kids feel capable of making things on their own. As Gareth Branwyn of Maker Media describes them, the books had "a sense of scientific rigor, an 'I can do this' hands-on allure, as well as a feeling of artfulness, creativity, and play that we'd never seen in a technical publication."[5]

The books embody Forrest's signature style: meticulous yet approachable, with an undercurrent of amateur mischief. *Getting Started in Electronics* feels as if it were written not by a teacher but by a precocious peer. The books explained; they did not condescend. And people of an impressionable age at that time appreciated that.

But Forrest's legacy is not all rainbows. There are some—at least, a vocal minority—who disdain Forrest Mims III. He's a DIY hero to some and a fraudulent nonscientist to others. He's a reminder that nothing troubles mainstream science more than an amateur out on his own.

※ ※ ※

There's one more thing you should know about Forrest Mims III: he's a creationist. He's a conservative Christian and a proponent of intelligent design. If you ask him, he'll tell you his creationist beliefs are evidence based—that he's found biological forms that don't fit Darwin's model—and that most biologists willfully ignore this evidence because it challenges their status quo.

He'll also tell you he prefers the term *superintelligent design* because the intelligence responsible for the creation of life is beyond any intelligence we can comprehend.[6]

Forrest's creationist beliefs came to light in 1988, when he bid for a prestigious writing position at *Scientific American*. He was short-listed to become the editor of the magazine's Amateur Scientist column—a column well known for detailing physics experiments readers could reproduce at home.

Forrest had all but secured the position. Then it arose during casual conversation with the magazine's editor, Jonathan Piel, that Forrest doubted Darwin's theory of evolution. Although two managing editors supported Forrest's bid for the position, the decision was ultimately Piel's. Piel ran three of Forrest's sample columns in the magazine but never hired him as an editor.

Armand Schwab Jr., one of the editors who supported Forrest's bid for the job, insisted Piel didn't doubt Forrest's ability to write the column. He simply feared the magazine would lose credibility with professional scientists if it employed an amateur who believed in the biblical account of creation.

"You have to understand," Schwab explained, "that creationism is sort of a shibboleth for scientists."[7] A shibboleth is a black mark—a telltale sign that someone is a fraud. If kept secret, the person can pass as part of the group. Once exposed, it's a dead giveaway that they don't belong.

This is a moment in the writing of this book when I have to check myself. I was raised to trust mainstream science. I was raised to understand that nothing can be proven beyond a shadow of a doubt in science, but if anything could be, it would be the theory of evolution through the process of natural selection. An astounding amount of evidence points toward it being a reality. And I, like many people, feel reflexive hostility toward anyone who would question it.

But then, this is exactly what amateurs are for.

Professionals become dangerous when they rely on *Just trust us, it's true.* Authority beyond question is a level of power professionals should not be allowed to have. Amateurs play an important role when they disagree, when they assert their independence, when they question what is not to be questioned, when they refuse to make the concessions required for acceptance. They may commit career suicide by stating their own opinions, but their willingness to disagree themselves out of a job does us all a service.

Professionals often act as if they've arrived at some objective truths about the world—about nature, human behavior, society, and the like. In *The Rise of Professionalism*, Magali Sarfatti Larson puts it bluntly when she says that because they invent truth, "all professionals are priests."[8]

But nothing known to humanity is really objective. Nothing is not interpreted. Even evidence, even data—everything is interpreted by a mind and its senses. You and I and Forrest the amateur are free to interpret too.

But you don't know what you're talking about, says the person who's frustrated by amateur interpretations. *That's fine,* I say to that person. *That's your interpretation of the amateur's interpretation.* The amateur's interpretation still gets to exist.

꙳ ꙳ ꙳

The *Scientific American* controversy became a defining event in Forrest's career. The *New York Times* and the *Washington Post* reported on it at the time as an example of how ideologically rigid mainstream science had become. To this day, when Forrest is interviewed, he's asked half-baked questions about his nonconformist beliefs. *Thanks for the RadioShack books,* people say, *but how can you seriously believe the Bible's account of creation?*

As for Forrest's response to the controversy, he just kept it moving. Once the media frenzy died down, he continued writing, publishing, tinkering, studying the atmosphere, and generally doing whatever he wanted to do. He did not appear to be shaken by the actions of *Scientific American*, perhaps because he didn't need the magazine to legitimize him. He would have enjoyed writing for the magazine, but that one job wouldn't have defined him. His actions indicate he'd rather think and speak freely than seek legitimacy.

To me, however, the magazine's actions have significance. Forrest, up until that point, had found substantial merit-based success. He did good work, and people judged him favorably based on his work. But the moment he diverged ideologically from the status quo, his lack of credentials seemed to matter. He was always an amateur, but suddenly he was an *amateur*. It makes me wonder if Jonathan Piel would have given him the job, all things considered, if he'd just had that *Dr.* before his name.

I pose the question to Forrest. "Did you ever think, later in life, that it'd be beneficial to go back and get a graduate degree in science?"

He thinks for a moment. "Well, I've published twenty-five or so papers in peer-reviewed science journals. Some of those papers could have been a PhD dissertation. But I always got to thinking, if I go back and get a PhD, I'm going to waste all that time taking courses I do not like."

"But it would have, I guess, greased the wheel in some situations. . . ."

He hums. "In my entire career, I have never been asked by any journal editor or any other scientist for that matter: 'What are your academic credentials?' 'What's your degree in?' 'What was your PhD thesis?'" he says. "I've only been asked about my papers. My research and my writing. So, what does that tell you about college? It tells me that my college education is completely worthless if all anyone cares about is what you've done. What you've published in a peer-reviewed, scholarly journal of science. That's what counts."

"So how do you get published in a peer-reviewed journal as an amateur?"

"After I published my first paper for *Nature*—that's the most famous science journal in the world, by the way—all these professional scientists called me and went 'Gosh, how do I get into *Nature*?' and I said, 'Well, you just gotta go out there and make a discovery!'"

Forrest Mims III, a man with a most complicated life, demonstrates for us the simplest reason one becomes a master amateur: because he can. Forrest realized early on that he was capable enough, resourceful enough, and bore enough intrinsic motivation to do science without becoming a professional scientist. He's no hero or fraud; he's not all "white hat" or "black hat." If anything, he's a lone ranger—a man who'd rather be free on the outside than safe on the inside.

OUT WHERE THE STATUS QUO CAN'T HURT YOU

Great master amateurs choose freedom over security. They fiercely guard their right to use their time and energy as they wish. They choose intellectual freedom over groupthink, and perhaps more importantly, they choose the literal freedom that comes from swearing no allegiances to any organizations.

I say this second choice is perhaps the more important one, because remaining outside professional organizations has real-world practical and financial consequences. It's harder to find your way all on your own. It can be harder to make a living on your own. But master amateurs choose to remain independent in part because they believe that intellectual freedom—freedom of thought and speech—only really exists in the literal freedom that comes from making no promises.

In other words, they take their lack of associations seriously. In true paradoxical form, they are committed to being noncommittal.

A great master amateur is committed to being noncommittal because she sees advantages in remaining an outsider by choice. She does *not* remain an outsider because she's not good enough to join the group. In fact, high-profile companies and professional associations often court master amateurs only to get repeatedly turned down.

Why would someone do this? What does an amateur gain by remaining out in a working wilderness? First of all, you gain self-reliance, and self-reliance is a requirement to becoming an expert at starting over. You can't become an expert at starting over if you've married yourself to a professional group or a fixed hierarchy of competence. Even if you someday felt compelled to start over, it would cost you too much. You'd have too much to lose. You'd resist starting over, even in those moments when you saw the tides of time turning and your group staying perilously still.

So, there's the fact that freedom is future-proofed. Having a self-contained career means you can throw it on your back and take it wherever you go. These lightweight careers give master amateurs their second advantage—the freedom to explore, and exploration leads them to bigger visions and better insights. There's a reason the cliché exists that outsiders have the greatest insights. You rarely get an unencumbered view of a landscape indoors; you see less of the world when you live in confines. Freedom is good for the future of ideas, and it's good for the working person's soul.

It's also good for the professions. They might be reticent to admit it, but knowledgeable outsiders push professional organizations to be better. While professional organizations (meaning groups of people with the same training using a common language to work toward common goals) serve a very important purpose, they need outside influence. They need outside perspectives. They need reminders that they're (in most cases) working for the public good. Only knowledgeable members of the public can provide that influence and perspective.

Think of it this way. If the world were a living organism, then a professional society is like a cell. It's enclosed by a membrane and functions well as a self-contained unit. The competent amateurs in this living organism are like free-floating nutrients. They permeate the cell's membrane and keep the cell healthy. They are not part of the cell; they are critical visitors. Indeed, the cell manages well in its enclosed state, but if it shuts itself off completely, it dies. The organism needs both: siloed, self-contained units *and* free-floating nutrients. Most importantly, it needs them to work together.

A great master amateur will learn how to permeate these boundaries—to influence professional groups and hold them accountable—without assimilating. They'll learn how to interact with a group without becoming part of it. Take Forrest as an example. He worked with professional scientists and professional organizations like NASA. He published articles in professional journals like *Nature*. But he never agreed—either implicitly or explicitly—to only think in a "professional" way.

When we talk about getting formal education, we know that means getting rigorous training, supervision, and a standardized body of knowledge. But there's another thing you get: indoctrination. Formal education is not just about teaching facts and techniques. It's also about teaching you to think the way the group wants you to think. It's about teaching you what to believe as well as what to know.

Forrest represents the amateur who, whether consciously or not, decides to forgo professional indoctrination. It's not just that he didn't major in science. It's more than that. He never went before a panel of group representatives and proved himself worthy. He never passed the authorities' tests or submitted to their requirements. As a result, he never swore allegiance to the governing body, and through his nonallegiance, he's free to come to his own conclusions.

Some will say his conclusions about evolution are terribly wrong. But the fact that he would even offer up his conclusions—that he would speak freely about his "terribly wrong" conclusions to a professional authority—shows just how free he is. I'm certain there are many professionals who believe things in opposition to their profession's status quo—and who would never say a word. Those silent professionals are choosing security. But at what cost?

Standing apart from the group, even when one could easily fit in, is a skill we could all stand to practice. It's a skill that promotes self-reliance, ethical whistle-blowing, and accountability in powerful groups.

Perhaps you can't live your whole life in a working wilderness. But every once in a while, take a look outside. When you feel the initiative to do something or say something outside the walls of your professional housing, consider it. If you notice yourself starting to suffocate from the status quo, go take a walk out where the status quo can't hurt you.

THE OLDEST AMATEUR

In 1991, the American Institute of Architects named Frank Lloyd Wright the greatest American architect of all time. The institute also named Fallingwater—Wright's iconic summer cottage named for its precarious placement on the lip of a waterfall—the best all-time work of American architecture.[9]

Frank Lloyd Wright is one of those icons, like Edison, whose dominance in his field was so great it's almost a cliché. Ask anybody on the street to name a great architect, and they'll probably say Frank Lloyd Wright, perhaps without even knowing why. He's a man, a myth, a legend: *the best architect ever.*

The thing is, according to those who should know better—the professional architects comprising the AIA—he actually *was* the best architect ever.

Frank Lloyd Wright spent seven eventful decades spreading his signature constructions across the United States. The ranch-style "Prairie" house he invented, with its wide-open interior, muted color palette, and flat-as-a-pancake roof, became the model midwestern home. He coined the term *organic* to describe how a man-made structure could be made to seem natural. He showed architects everywhere how to bring the outdoors inside. He invented the first American design aesthetic and, in doing so, changed forever the way Americans live.

Wright designed over a thousand structures in his lifetime—a lifetime begun at the end of the Civil War and ended at the beginning of the space age. Of those one thousand designs, he brought 532 buildings to life. In addition to his apple-pie midwestern homes, he built a handful of conceptual masterpieces. There's Fallingwater, his organic magnum opus. There's also the Ennis House in Los Angeles, a modern-day Mayan temple made famous as a postapocalyptic apartment in the movie *Blade Runner*. Then there's the Guggenheim Museum in New York City, a building that looks like a filleted marshmallow on Fifth Avenue.

What, can we speculate, made Frank Lloyd Wright so prolific *and* inventive? Some credit his spartan upbringing at the hands of Welsh immigrants in the frigid Wisconsin countryside. His childhood gave him grit; he'd sometimes describe it as bleak, with the shining light being his favorite toy—a set of maple-wood building blocks.

Others credit his gritty inventiveness to his lifelong love of hands-on experience. After high school, he enrolled in a civil-engineering program at the University of Wisconsin only to drop out after a year to work as a draftsman in Chicago. He'd later say that "true study is a form of experience" and mock formal education as a "trampling of the herd."[10]

Wright spent six years working as a draftsman and apprentice in Chicago, then spent another decade working under the radar as an independent contractor. His breakout opportunity came in 1905 at the age of thirty-eight, when the Unitarian Universalist church that he and his family attended burned to the ground. Wright bid for and won the right to reconstruct the building in his own style. His church, Unity Temple, would later be called "the first modern building in the world."[11]

The design of Unity Temple was pure sacrilege. Wright built his church, pew to pulpit, in the least divine material possible: reinforced concrete. He built, in no uncertain terms, a concrete block. The building had no front door; congregants had to go around the back to enter. The walls had no windows. Instead, Wright hoisted stained-glass windows into the ceiling.

Ostensibly, he said, these design elements reduced street noise. The effect, however, was that once one entered the church, one's eyes were drawn naturally up to heaven.

Today, architects use industrial materials like concrete in residential buildings all the time. The commonplaceness of this material nowadays can be directly credited to Unity Temple.

After Unity Temple's construction, Wright gained notoriety and a healthy income bump. He did not necessarily gain leadership in his profession. The more successful he became, the more he kept architecture—the profession—at arm's length. He never went back to get a degree, nor did he ever accept a position in academia. He adamantly refused to join the American Institute of Architects (ironically, the same professional body that'd later name him "best of all time"), slamming it with statements like "I would do anything [the institute] asked me for, except join them to make a harbor of refuge for the incompetent."[12]

Instead, Wright continued to innovate on his own. In 1910, he completed the residence that'd epitomize his "Prairie" style: the Robie House. The home of Frederick and Lora Robie of Hyde Park, Chicago, was a sprawling brick-and-mortar shelter dressed down in burnt browns and tans. It was planted in long rectangles that hugged the ground, echoing the open plains. Its cantilevered roof extended well past the exterior walls, looming large like a clear sky.

The Robie House ushered in a new look for single-family homes—one that made no reference to classical Greece or Victorian England or the French countryside. But the home's true innovation lay inside its walls. Wright used the Robie's big budget to construct the building's frame from steel, a material thought too costly to use in homes at the time. The hidden steel beams supported the whole weight of the house, making interior walls optional. Support columns within rooms became obsolete. Exterior walls bore little weight, allowing for floor-to-ceiling windows. The result was a free and open interior space bathed in natural light—the first open-floor plan.

The Robie House shot Wright onto a higher plain of influence, one he would inhabit—with the occasional scandal-induced dip—for the next five decades of his life. In 1949, the American Institute of Architects, perhaps feeling pressure to instate Wright before he was gone, awarded him their highest honor: the AIA Gold Medal. Wright remained unmoved. When asked to comment on Frank Lloyd Wright's perpetual cold shoulder, then AIA president Douglas Orr said: "Mr. Wright has always been a lone wolf. He was not one given to joining associations."[13]

Well into his old age, people continued to nag architecture's lone wolf. *Why?* they'd ask. *Why not just join?* In 1956, NBC reporter Joseph Meyers finally captured Wright's answer.

"Because," he said, "I believe less and less in professionalism as I see it practiced. I think it's a kind of refined gangsterism . . . The architectural profession is all that's the matter with architecture. Why should I join them?"

Then, drifting into a past conversation he'd had with publishing tycoon Henry Luce, an eighty-eight-year-old Frank Lloyd Wright said: "As Henry Luce said in astonishment: 'Are you an old amateur?' And I said, 'Yes, Mr. Luce. I am the oldest.'"[14]

THE LIMITS BY WHICH YOU LIVE

The desire for freedom and independence is the simplest reason one chooses a life of amateurism. It hardly needs explanation. It's an innate human impulse—the itch to be free.

But freedom is not the easiest choice nowadays; our current work culture encourages us to institutionalize ourselves. First there's college—the gateway drug of institutions—the first group we're told we must join if we're to have a halfway-decent life. Then we graduate and immediately pick our next institution: company, firm, agency, government, or more school.

These institutions act for us like stepping-stones in the water—a safe place to stand while the world rushes past. We start to panic when we can't see where the next stone is, as if we may drown. The silly thing is . . . we could also just swim.

I don't want to disparage institutions too much. There are undeniable benefits to joining a group. Groups provide structure, focus, and a sense of identity. If you do choose to swim instead of skip, you'll face the hard task of providing these essential supports for yourself.

Hopefully this book helps you on the identity front. You are (or can be) a master amateur.

On the structure and focus fronts, Forrest Mims and Frank Lloyd Wright have something in common that I think reveals how they provided these supports for themselves. That commonality is: they both stuck to one big pursuit. For Forrest, that pursuit was new technological and scientific discoveries. For Wright, it was an American form of architecture.

Both men, in a certain way, limited themselves in order to be free. Each narrowed his own path through the wilderness so he wouldn't get lost. Each defined his own vocational boundary instead of letting a community do it for him. And within these self-made boundaries, they were free to do whatever they wanted.

There's a term for this. It's *creative constraints*. It describes the fact that people are better at finding creative solutions to a problem when the problem has some limitations. In other words, setting some limits frees up the mind. The question is: Will you set the limits by which you live, or will you let others do it for you?

The ability to apply *one's own* constraints to free up one's own mind is a core competency of a master amateur. It's the skill that makes the status quo powerless in his presence. It's the thing that makes a master amateur look at the professional ranks and ask—with no answer in sight—*Why should I join them?*

CHAPTER 6

DIVERSITY

A lot of different flowers make a bouquet.
—Islamic proverb

A WELL-BALANCED PORTFOLIO

In the years spent researching and writing this book, I read countless articles about amateurism. Most, however, were not about amateurism so named. Some were about the "side-hustle" phenomenon, while others were about "slash careers." Still others were about the "gig economy" or the "maker movement." Some focused on the disconnect between higher education and workforce demands. Others warned of Big Media's increasing reliance on user-generated content.

An amateur by any other name, I'd think and read, *would smell as sweet.*

I can't say if the authors of these pieces omitted the word *amateur* on purpose. Perhaps they just weren't thinking about their topic in that way. But as I read more and more, I started to wonder. Are these newfangled work trends not new at all—just old-fashioned amateurism repackaged for sale? Is what we're calling the "future of work" a lot more like the "past of work" than we realize?

Intent to find an answer, I tracked down a man who writes extensively about the future of work and asked him.

℘ ℘ ℘

On April 25, 2017, Kabir Sehgal published a think piece on the website of the *Harvard Business Review* entitled "Why You Should Have (at Least) Two Careers." In it, he laid out the logic behind one of the most popular "new work" trends: the "portfolio career." He argued that work is not a zero-sum game, and too many people quit a perfectly good day job to pursue a dream job when they could feasibly do both.

Not only *could* they do both, Kabir argued; they *should* do both. Why? Because multiple careers are mutually beneficial. By doing both, you'll learn skills in one career that apply to the other. You'll meet people in one industry who can help you in the other. You'll find enough time to eat and sleep, Kabir insisted, and you'll feel more fulfilled. "Two careers are better than one," he wrote. "And by committing to two careers, you will produce benefits for both."[1]

Kabir doesn't just write about the portfolio career—he lives it. He maintains not one, not two, not three, but four concurrent careers. First, he's a corporate strategist for a Fortune 500 company (his "day job") and previously held a VP position at J. P. Morgan. Then he's a music producer. He's produced albums for jazz and Latin-music legends Arturo O'Farrill and the Ted Nash Big Band. For his work as a music producer, Kabir has won four Grammys and two Latin Grammys.

Then he's an author. He's penned five nonfiction books on topics as varied as music, democracy, civil rights, and money. *Coined: The Rich Life of Money and How Its History Has Shaped*

Us tells the story of money from ancient barter systems to present-day Bitcoin. It made both the *New York Times* and *Wall Street Journal* bestseller lists in 2015. He's also authored a handful of bestselling children's books.

And last but not least, Kabir's a decorated military veteran and lieutenant in the US Navy Reserve.

We can glean from his resume that Kabir has exceptional organizational and time-management skills. So, when I contact him to discuss his portfolio career, I'm determined to not even ask about those things. *How do you get it all done?* It's an interesting-enough question, and one I suspect people ask him all the time. But having read much of Kabir's writing, I know the answer is simple. He gets it all done by just getting it all done.

Instead, I want to ask him, *Why do you get it all done?* Why, if given the chance, wouldn't one cash that VP-level check and chill?

And I want to ask him: *Don't parallel-tracked careers create a certain inevitability—that inevitability being amateurism?* One can't realistically be a "professional" at four or five things at once. Kabir is certainly a professional in his financial-services day job, as he holds a master's degree from the London School of Economics. *But aren't you,* I intend to ask him, *an amateur at everything else?*

☙ ☙ ☙

Kabir and I connect over the phone on a Monday, 12:30 p.m. sharp. I suspect he's on his lunch break—making use of every hour. Even the halves. A touch of wind in his voice suggests he's walking around the block, probably in one of the fine silk suits he wears to his day job. I sense I don't have much time with him, so I open the floor.

"Tell me how it all happened," I say. "How did you end up with one of the fattest portfolio careers out there?"

Not one to waste time, Kabir skips his childhood completely and starts his story in college. He attended Dartmouth College in New Hampshire, where he, by his own admission, rarely went to class. Instead, he spent much of his time working on the 2004 John Kerry presidential campaign. The campaign primary was in full effect, and New Hampshire was a critical state for Kerry to carry. Kabir, along with an army of volunteers, knocked down New Hampshire doors and helped Kerry land the Democratic nomination.

At the same time (and still in lieu of going to class), Kabir was touring with famed jazz trumpeter Wynton Marsalis. A jazz bassist since childhood, Kabir had won a music competition in high school that happened to be sponsored by Wynton, and the two had kept in touch.

He'd oscillate, as he describes it, between these two worlds: one week spent in campaign politics, the next in live music. He became adaptable to these different environments. And to his surprise, he became known in each world for being in the other. "The funny thing was," he tells me, "when I was with the Kerry campaign, all they wanted to talk about was music. And when I was with Wynton, all they wanted to talk about was politics."

Kabir instinctively became an intermediary—a translator—between these two worlds. While in one camp, he'd find himself translating the world of the other camp into terms his current camp could understand. He became, as he puts it, "an evangelist for the other." "I've found that this played out through all my careers," he says. "I'm able to play the 'other' and bring something new to the conversation."

ॐ ॐ ॐ

After graduating from Dartmouth and the London School of Economics, Kabir tried founding a technology startup ("It was supposed to be 'Facebook for India,'" he says with a chuckle) and quickly ran out of money. He decided he needed to put diversions aside and settle down into the career for which he'd trained: investment banking. He joined J. P. Morgan first in San Francisco, then in the Wall Street shark tank of New York. The job was tough at first. It demanded long hours, yet many of those hours were wasted on stodgy formalities.

Kabir was treading water, unsure that a life behind a desk would ever make him happy. Until, over time, he realized the job wasn't really about putting in hours. It wasn't about making courtesy calls or even managing assets. It was about forming relationships. If he could connect with his clients in a unique way, he surmised, he could meet the job's demands *and* reclaim some of his time.

"Once I realized it was a relationship-driven job," he recalls, "I had to enhance those relationships. I started finding people who had similar interests to me on Wall Street— politics, music—and they became my clients."

In other words, the extracurricular activities Kabir had placed on a back burner in an attempt to "adult" became the opening wedge in his financial-services career. His hobbies humanized him in the frosty world of banking. Perhaps more importantly, they made him just a little bit different.

On Wall Street, everyone is a "finance guy." Even the women, in attitude and philosophy, are finance guys. Everyone has similar educational backgrounds and similar perspectives. "Taken together," Kabir once wrote in an article, "all of us establish a 'consensus' view on the markets."[2] But most financial-services clients hankered for something different. "Give me a contrarian perspective," Kabir wrote of them saying. Kabir, being just *that much* different—with a foot sticking out of their professional bubble—became the guy to provide that contrarian perspective.

During his years at J. P. Morgan, Kabir's trademarked "evangelism for the other" earned him high-profile clients, a VP-level position, and more time to do what he wanted. He wrote five books during this period, mostly by finding time in the middle of the day. "I became sort of antisocial," he admits. "During lunch I'd go to the New York Public Library and write. I negotiated with my boss so that I could leave early and not come in for morning meetings. My relationships with my clients were so strong—meaning I was bringing in a substantial amount of revenue—that I could do that."

Then something interesting happened. The more he wrote and produced music on the side, the more his side-hustles spilled over onto his day job. In turn, his day job spilled right back.

He'd produce an album, share it with his clients, and some of those clients would offer to fund his next album. Now with funding, he'd land a bigger-name artist to work with on his next album. With a bigger-name artist to endorse him, he'd land a bigger publishing deal for his next book. The book would land him bigger-deal clients. And so on and so forth.

This is what portfolio-careerists mean by "mutually beneficial." This, I've come to understand, is the answer to my first question: *Why do you do it all?* Because multiple careers create momentum that a single profession can't.

Professions move linearly from point A to point B. And it's usually the force of an individual's will that determines how close he or she gets to point B.

Portfolio careers don't move from point A to point B. They swirl.

One's day job and side-hustles move together, forming a whirlpool of success. If maintained, the whirlpool generates power beyond the efforts of the individual. He can set the virtuous cycle in motion and start to ride.

ഗ്ര ഗ്ര ഗ്ര

At this point in our conversation, I offer Kabir an observation. "It seems to me like you use your side projects as leverage for your day job and vice versa."

"Definitely," he responds. "For example, I wrote *Coined*—my book about money—partially because I was thinking, 'Well, I could give a client a business card, or I could give him my book on the history and future of money.'" He pauses. I hear a siren wail and fade on his end of the line. "I definitely think of my books and music as investments in my whole career," he finishes.

This makes intuitive sense to someone working in the financial sector. In finance, there's stability in diversity; a diversified portfolio is a safer investment, on the whole, than a nondiversified one. Any one holding might flop, but the others will float the failures. *Why*, Kabir seems to suggest, *should this only apply to investing? Why wouldn't it also apply to life?*

"Did you ever consider quitting your day job once your side projects started succeeding?" I ask him.

Kabir hums, and I realize I'm still living under the assumption that one would happily abandon a day job if their dream job took off. He reminds me it's not one or the other. "Having a day job actually makes the side projects easier, I think, because you have a paycheck. You can finance your creative projects, and you can support other people's projects too."

"And," he adds, "worrying about getting paid taxes your creativity."

So, Kabir keeps his day job, despite his Grammys and bestsellers. I find this an interesting choice, even by master-amateur standards. Most of the master amateurs I've profiled in this book choose to free up as much of their time as possible, even at the cost of financial security. They prioritize time over money (with the probable exception of Matt Monahan, since he loves money).

But Kabir is uniquely untroubled by limited time, so he prioritizes money. He constrains himself where a constraint fits him best—on time. It would certainly not fit everyone best; many of us would freak out trying to do all that Kabir does. But it's a constraint he designed for himself based on his own strengths. And with it in place, he frees up his finances and, by extension, his creativity.

"You must make some sacrifices having so little free time," I insist.

"I have disengaged from a lot of social life," he says. "I've found that hanging out with the people I'm doing projects with is really exciting. So when a friend says, 'Hey let's go watch a football game this weekend,' I'm like, 'And do what?'"

"I'm sure they love that," I tease.

"Well, I don't get invited anymore." He chuckles. "But it's fine. We'll reconnect when the time is right."

Kabir's breath steadies, and I sense he's no longer walking. It's 1:00 p.m. sharp, and he's gotta go back to work.

"Kabir," I blurt, "some of these things you call your careers . . . aren't you really an amateur at them?"

"I'm probably an amateur at everything I do," he states.

"Do you think having a portfolio career is just being a perpetual amateur?"

"Well, being a professional assumes you're a subject-matter expert and have this depth of knowledge in one thing. But if you skate across lanes, you're an amateur at each individual thing, but you're a professional at connecting those things. That becomes an expertise: combining different things together to make something new."

I thank Kabir for his time and hang up the phone. I'm pleased to know that Kabir Sehgal—king of the portfolio career, lord of the side-hustle, passionate advocate of new work—is also an amateur mastering one of the core competencies of the future: mixing together different disciplines to make something new.

NEW SOMETHINGS

Some of the most successful master amateurs forgo a linear career in favor of a diversified one. They mix and match disciplines to make something new. That "something new" could be a new invention, a new solution, a new application, a new job, a new industry—a new insight. Whatever "new something" comes from their work, these diversified master amateurs are actually working in a way that's rather ancient. They're learning things they don't already know and doing things they don't already know how to do.

In practical terms, the diversified master amateur might maintain multiple careers in parallel, à la the portfolio career. She might rapid-cycle through different jobs in different industries—an intentional dabbler—with an endgame in mind of eventually putting them together in her own way. She might apply a "formal" expertise she's gained—like computer science or design or sport—to an unrelated topic. In doing so, she picks up ideas developed over there and brings them over here.

She's the most essential worker bee: the kind that cross-pollinates industries.

She will probably, no matter what, supplement her primary work with side endeavors to elevate her career as a whole. These side-hustles may complement her primary work, or they may, on the surface, seem irrelevant. They may even contradict her primary work. The contradictory side-hustle is the best of all hustles, in my opinion, because contradiction is fertile ground for new somethings. And over time, commonalities emerge. They won't remain contradictions for long.

In this way, master amateurs expand their careers instead of contracting them. Let's say, for example, a woman has a day job in real estate. On the side, she runs a small sustainable farm. Over the decades, through independent research and raising her own children, she's become highly knowledgeable about children's education. She also writes.

You can see how each activity has some level of overlap with the others, and they can do more in tandem than they can apart. In essence, each is part of a larger machine: her vocation. Real estate is the wheel that keeps the gears turning. Farming and children's education are the lever and pulley, respectively. Writing is the wedge that opens new opportunities. The machine does more than the parts do on their own—it raises her to new heights. Instead of a profession, this master amateur has a vocation that's more than the sum of its parts.

℘ ℘ ℘

This competency of the future—mixing different disciplines to make something new—can seem intimidating, but it's quite simple in practice. You don't have to set out trying to invent something new. If you expose yourself to different disciplines, new somethings will happen naturally.

But to be fair, the act of exposing yourself to disciplines other than your own can be hard. In the past, the main challenge was access. If you weren't "in" that discipline, your access to its vaults would be limited. Today, with the internet, access to information is less of an issue. Instead, the main barrier you have to overcome is social pressure to specialize.

These days, being "well rounded" is for the young. The moment you step out of high school, you're pressured to name your specialty. If you're privileged, this pressure to specialize starts even younger. The older you get, the sharper and less round you're expected to be. It's an insult at a certain age to be called a jack-of-all-trades, because we know what comes next. Master of none.

Nonmaster. Nonexpert. Nonprofessional. A career defined in the negative.

This isn't just amorphous social pressure. It *is* harder to get traditional jobs as a generalist; nearly all job descriptions are written for specialists. In fact, being highly specialized is probably the easiest path to getting a traditional job. Assuming, that is, that your specialty doesn't suddenly disappear due to globalization or technology.

This is the first problem with having a single specialization: it could vanish, leaving you to start over from scratch. The second problem is: the more you boil down your knowledge base to a thick reduction, the more you know only what you know. And the more you know only what you know, the more you actually start to know very little.

Exposure is the decision to reverse this reductionist trend. It's the brave decision to start getting to know what you don't know.

༄ ༄ ༄

As Kabir demonstrates, exposure to different disciplines takes time. Sometimes, it also takes money. But it pays dividends. It gives the mind things to think about other than what it always thinks about. It opens the door to an obligatory skill of the future: interdisciplinary thinking.

Now, no one is so isolated that they don't think between disciplines on occasion. The special thing about master amateurs is that interdisciplinary thinking is not their exception; it's their rule. It's routine to them—something they're doing more often than they're not. It's one of their day-to-day tasks, as normal as paying bills or checking email. When something is so routine, it no longer takes effort. Once the effort wanes, the new somethings emerge.

In another time, a person who mastered interdisciplinary thinking and invented new somethings was called a Renaissance man. The archetype, Leonardo da Vinci, had a portfolio career if there ever was one. He was a painter, inventor, anatomist, and engineer, to name a few of his careers. More impressively, perhaps, he routinely blurred—to the point of erasure—the lines among these disciplines.

A few centuries after Leonardo da Vinci's life, Renaissance men started being called polymaths (from the Greek *poly*, "much," and *manthanein*, "to learn"). Literally, "one who has learned much."

The archetypal polymath was Benjamin Franklin: inventor, physicist, politician, publisher, and raunchy comedian. He never let a lack of foreknowledge get in his way; if he wanted to explore something, he explored. Writer Jack Hitt, in his book *Bunch of Amateurs*, singled out Benjamin Franklin as the ultimate polymath, "meta-pioneer," and original American amateur. Franklin optimized, Hitt wrote, "the down-to-earth philosophy of the dabbler fooling around in search of a working solution."[3]

In theory, we admire polymaths and Renaissance people—we use these monikers as praise. In theory, we want more Leonardo da Vincis and Ben Franklins in society. But in practicality, we don't give their modern-day equivalents many opportunities. We don't make it easy for people to remain diversified and survive.

What job—realistically—would Leo or Ben be qualified to do today? If they were searching an online job board, what section would they scroll to? What would their LinkedIn headline be? "Jack of All Trades, Master of Amateurism"?

❧ ❧ ❧

Here's a quick anecdote. Way back in 1515, Leonardo da Vinci met the king of France, whose name (appropriately enough) was King Francis I. Upon meeting, King Francis—knowing only of Leonardo's prowess as a painter—immediately asked Leo to move to France and design the French military's machines of war.

The king offered Leo this job (which came with the marvelous title of Premier Painter and Engineer and Architect to the King) based on Leo's excellence in an *unrelated* discipline.[4] Think of how weird that would be today. It would be practically unthinkable. "That's like the Department of Defense calling up Georgia O'Keeffe during the Cold War," journalist Jeff Goins once wrote for *Fast Company*, "asking her to consult on developing thermonuclear weapons. It just wouldn't happen."[5]

No, it wouldn't. Because the world today wants you to stay in your lane.

But what if it could happen?

What if, given the chance, anyone could cross disciplines?

What if everyone has the potential to be "one who has learned much"?

What if everyone has a perfect combination of interests—lying dormant—to invent an important new something?

You could argue that Leonardo da Vinci and Benjamin Franklin were just special—that they were geniuses in addition to being Renaissance men and polymaths. That may be true. But I suspect everyone has a little Ben and Leo in them. I think *Jack of All Trades, Master of Amateurism* is ripe to become a popular job title soon enough.

To prove that discipline-crossing is for everyone, I'll now tell you the stories of two exceptionally normal people who crossed a discipline chasm to contribute something new.

SEEING IN THE DARK

In 1927, on the outskirts of a nondescript Illinois town, sixteen-year-old Grote Reber received his amateur radio license, numbered W9GFZ. The curious teenager (with the even more curious name) pinged close to sixty countries with his ham radio during the years he grew to adulthood. By age twenty-two, Grote had earned a BS in electrical engineering from the Armour Institute (now called the Illinois Institute of Technology). By twenty-five, he'd found work as an engineer at the Stewart-Warner radio factory in Chicago—his day job, a very good one by Depression-era standards. At twenty-seven, he'd bargained with his mother for use of a plot of land in her backyard, on which he built a radio dish aimed at space. And by twenty-nine, he had illuminated the dark universe.

Grote Reber—professional engineer, amateur radio operator, and amateur astronomer—was the first person to map the radio sky. He was first to conduct a successful survey of the cosmos in the radio frequency, illuminating the vast swathes of space that emit little to no visible light. In fact, he was the first to even try. And in trying without knowing what would happen, he almost single-handedly opened up darkness to scientific study.

His life as the first and (for about a decade) only radio astronomer began in 1937, after Grote read an article about Karl Jansky's discovery of radio static emanating from the Milky Way. Jansky made the discovery by accident while troubleshooting an annoying hissing sound that people were hearing over their Bell Labs telephones at certain hours of the day. Since the discovery was made in the context of industry and not science, no professional scientists took note of it.

But when Grote read about it, he sensed that this "star noise"—as Jansky called it—had scientific importance. Despite being an amateur astronomer (or perhaps because he was an amateur astronomer), he simply knew it must. "So," Grote would later describe, "I consulted with myself and decided to build a dish."[6]

The dish that Grote Reber built by hand in his mother's backyard became the second-ever radio telescope, and the first to utilize the now-standard parabolic shape (think of the giant SETI telescopes Jodie Foster lies beside in the movie *Contact*). Grote's parabolic dish spread thirty-two feet in diameter and focused its transmission onto a radio antenna that projected twenty feet into the air.

He spent his own money—acquired through his day job—to buy the parts to build the dish. He determined the dish's design and dimensions by reading optics books that he checked out from the public library. He reasoned that higher radio frequencies would pick up more detail, providing more information about the static's origin. So, relying heavily on his skills as an engineer, Grote built a dish that captured Jansky's star noise at a frequency 160 times higher than Jansky did.

At first (this should surprise no one at this point), the professional astronomy community dismissed Grote's findings. When asked, Grote said he felt this rejection was less about him being an amateur and more a result of his work falling between two fields: astronomy and radio engineering.

Radio engineers didn't care about *where* radio waves came from; they saw radio waves as a means of communication only.

Astronomers—the more dismissive group of the two—did not already know how radio waves were relevant to astronomy and therefore weren't open to considering how they might be. They weren't open to getting to know what they didn't already know. Grote once remarked that the astronomers he met "could not dream up any rational way by which the radio waves [from space] could be generated, and since they didn't know of a process, the whole affair was [to them] at best a mistake and at worst a hoax."[7]

Grote, untroubled by the "hoax" accusation, built a new, more precise dish in 1941 and set himself the task of mapping the entire sky in the radio frequency.

Within two years, his "sky map" was complete, and one professional astronomer started to take notice. His name was Otto Struve, and he was the editor of *Astrophysical Journal*. Struve, intrigued, sent Grote's map to a number of astronomers as well as a couple of radio engineers, but none reviewed it. The astronomers thought it was a work of radio engineering; the radio engineers thought it was astronomy.

Finally, Struve personally asked two astrophysicists, Louis Henyey and Philip Keenan, to visit Grote in Illinois and review his data. They went and concluded that Grote's data was reliable, professional grade, and important. With that, Struve published Grote's map of the dark in *Astrophysical Journal* the next year, and a new branch of scientific study was born.

The publication of Grote Reber's map led to an explosion of interest in radio astronomy after World War II. By midcentury, radio waves had allowed astrophysicists to detect black holes (objects long theorized to exist but never observed) as well as witness the birth and death of stars—events too chaotic to make sense of using visible light. And radio waves are by no means done making space comprehensible to us. They are expected to play a critical role in solving the spooky space mysteries known as dark matter and dark energy.

When asked by *Sky & Telescope* magazine in 1988 why he and not a professional astronomer was the one to map the radio sky, Grote chalked it up to knowing the right combination of things. He did not know more than astronomers knew about astronomy—far from it. But, he said, "I knew immensely more about astronomy than the astronomers knew about electrical engineering."[8]

In other words, Grote Reber—an amateur—did not know more information than his professional counterparts. He knew more *different* information, and that opened up different opportunities to him. He was by nobody's account a genius. Instead, his genius was his particular mix of passions. His unique mix of interests made him the most qualified person to go find what was hidden in the dark.

THREADING THE NEEDLE

On a thoroughly average day back in 2001, Baltimore hairdresser Janet Stephens found herself with some time to kill. It was too early to pick up her daughter from music class, so Janet decided to go to a museum. She strolled the museum halls without plan, letting the fates guide her. Suddenly, somewhere amid the classical antiquities, Janet saw marble Greco-Roman statues milling around a big empty room like attendees of a lukewarm cocktail party.

The room, she found out, was being renovated. And the marble portrait statues—normally strung up on pedestals against the walls—were temporarily viewable up close and from all angles.

For Janet Stephens, this was the chance of a lifetime. She was a longtime history buff and professional hairdresser for over twenty-five years, but this was her first opportunity to see the back of an ancient woman's head. She'd always wondered how ancient women got their ornate hairstyles to hold together. "As I circled the portraits," she'd later tell a reporter, "I saw the logic of the hairstyles and determined to try some at home."[9]

Janet started with the elaborately braided bun of second-century Roman empress Julia Domna. She braided the long locks of her practice mannequin with ease and molded the braids into a type of bun that resembled a sourdough loaf. But when it came time to secure the bun to the head, nothing could get it to hold. Not hairpins, not hair spray. No matter what Janet did, it just kept falling apart.

So, Janet got to researching. She pored over images of Hellenistic busts. She scoured art-exhibition catalogs and read thick archaeology textbooks about Roman life, searching the footnotes for clues. It helped that she knew Italian and that her husband was a professor at Johns Hopkins University, granting her library privileges. Even so, it took Janet four years of independent research to make a breakthrough. And in the process, she became the world's first, and quite possibly only, "hairdo archaeologist."

൙ ൙ ൙

Janet's breakthrough went something like this. While studying translations of Roman literature, she learned that professional archaeologists believed these "impossible" hairstyles were wigs. Janet knew instinctively this was wrong.

First of all, ancient people didn't have synthetic fibers, which is what most wigs are made of today. And if every elite woman in the Roman empire wore a wig made of human hair, where was all this hair coming from? The ancient hair trade (if there ever was such a thing) would have been huge business—on par with gold and textiles. So where was the money trail?

These women had to be styling their natural hair, Janet was sure. There was just some critical component the professionals had missed. She suspected that archaeologists, not being hairdressers, had a limited frame of reference when it came to hair. They were probably misinterpreting something in the literature—she just didn't know what.

Then, in 2005, she found it: the Latin term *acus*. Ancient Roman women used *acus* to mean "needle and thread." Archaeologists, however, didn't see how "needle and thread" made sense in the context of hairdressing, so they translated it to "hairpin."

To Janet, however, "needle and thread" made infinitely more sense.

Julia Domna's braids couldn't be pinned to her head—Janet knew this from firsthand experience. But perhaps they could be *woven onto* her head with a needle and thread.

Janet tried out her theory on her practice mannequin, and it worked. In 2007, she submitted her findings to the *Journal of Roman Archaeology*. In her paper, she asserted that ancient Roman women did not wear wigs and did not style their hair with hairpins but rather "stitched" their hair into place. The journal performed its own experiments and determined that Janet was right. It published her paper the next year under the title "Ancient Roman Hairdressing: On (Hair)Pins and Needles."

"It's amazing how much chutzpah you have when you have no idea what you're doing," she told the *Wall Street Journal* upon the paper's publication. "I don't write scholarly material. I'm a hairdresser."[10]

The journal's editor, however, gave Janet far more credit. "I could tell even from the first version [of the paper] that it was a very serious piece of experimental archaeology which no scholar who was not a hairdresser—in other words, no scholar—would have been able to write."

Marden Nichols, a former assistant curator of ancient art at the Baltimore museum where Janet first gained her inspiration, agreed. "Like many classicists," Nichols said, "I spend my days analyzing works of literature and art that relate to activities I have never performed: harvesting crops, building temples, sacrificing animals."[11] Janet made a truly original contribution to this field, Nichols implied, precisely *because* she spent her days doing something outside it.

Janet succeeded in the scholarly realm of archaeology, not in spite of her unrelated background but because of it. She did not help a profession along despite being an amateur. She helped a profession along *because* she was an amateur.

Janet Stephens continues her work at the forefront of hairdo archaeology—the discipline she invented by mixing her interests together. In 2012, she demonstrated her Julia Domna recreation at the Archaeological Institute of America's annual conference in Philadelphia, using only period-appropriate tools. She returned to the conference the next year and became the first person ever to re-create the hairstyle of the vestal virgins on a modern-day person's head.

Janet has also taken her passion online. She has a popular YouTube channel where she teaches her loyal following of thirty-seven thousand subscribers how to re-create the hairstyles of their ancient feminine heroines—Cleopatra, Empress Faustina the Younger, and many more—with unparalleled historical accuracy.

And last but not least, Janet works as a hairdresser at Baltimore's Studio 921 Salon and Day Spa.

WE CONTAIN MULTITUDES

Earlier in this chapter, I said there are two things you have to do to become a modern-day polymath a.k.a. Renaissance person a.k.a. master amateur. First, you have to reverse the trend toward specialization and expose yourself to a number of diverse disciplines. Then you have to give your mind the freedom to think between those disciplines. You have to compare, contrast, and combine with abandon.

This expansive, flexible thinking is a generation engine for new somethings. It's also a prerequisite for master-amateur status and one of the most important survival skills of the future.

Now, I want to add a third thing you have to do. At the risk of sounding trite, you have to not worry about what people think of you. Or what they think of what you're doing. If you go this route, you'll end up doing work that people—by definition—won't immediately get. If they immediately get it, it's not really all that new.

So, for a while you may be the only one doing your particular work mix. For a decade or so, you may be the only radio astronomer on Earth, as Grote Reber was. That doesn't mean it'll always be that way.

You may get snickers when you announce your made-up job title. You may be mocked for saying you're a "forensic smartphone hacker" or "food stylist" or "animal acupuncturist" (all real jobs, by the way). I bet some of you snickered when I said Janet Stephens was a "hairdo archaeologist." That's okay—it's human nature to scorn something you don't immediately get. This will happen to you too.

But I bet that when you heard Janet's story, you found respect for her. People will find respect for you too.

And remember, even the most successful master amateurs deal with other people's inability to comprehend their work. Just last year, an interviewer from the *Harvard Business Review* asked Kabir if his career makes sense even to him, implying, of course, that his career makes no sense.

"It doesn't make sense to me, I just do it," he replied to the interviewer. "Do I contradict myself?" Kabir then said, paraphrasing Walt Whitman. "Yes. I contain multitudes."[12]

CHAPTER 7

ANGER

> *If you're not angry, you're not paying attention.*
> —Activist slogan

A CERTAIN SORT OF PTSD

By all accounts, the early-morning hours of Tuesday, September 11, 2001, were pristinely beautiful in Lower Manhattan. The sky had never been clearer. That same sky was slightly overcast outside the bite-sized town of Shanksville, Pennsylvania, and as still as a lake in Arlington, Virginia.

At 8:46 that Tuesday morning, a series of hijacked planes started swinging like wrecking balls across those skies, raining down dust and drywall and concrete onto unsuspecting cement below. It rained the bitterest, driest rain in Lower Manhattan.

The attacks on September 11, 2001, killed 2,996 people on the spot and injured at least six thousand more. Those killed were sleepy travelers, salary men and women, and first responders. They were heroes, victims, and bystanders. Parents, sons, and daughters. Those affected were also you and me, who even now—eighteen years later—still taste the residue of trauma done that day to the American heart, lung, and mind.

Not so far from ground zero, a seventeen-year-old boy named Dylan Avery watched the attacks unfold from his high school in upstate New York. He didn't know it then, but four years later he'd independently produce the movie that'd forever place doubt on the government's version of the events of 9/11. The movie was called *Loose Change*, and it would go on to become, in terms of viewership and cultural impact, the most successful viral video the internet has ever known.

Stylistically, *Loose Change* is like a confrontational MTV music video. It pairs news footage and still photographs from 9/11 with Dylan's flat narration and a relentless loop of hip-hop beats. In terms of content, the movie is mostly Dylan asking questions—questions to which he can find no answers.

Why did World Trade Center Building 7 collapse when it was not hit by a plane? Why was incredibly little plane wreckage found at the Pentagon? How is it physically possible that the World Trade Center towers fell at free-fall speed? Why was thermite, an explosive used to demolish buildings, found in the dust that suffocated Lower Manhattan?

The film, in asking these questions, suggests that 9/11 might have been an inside job—a crime aided or covered up by the US government to justify war abroad and espionage at home. The film insinuates a conspiracy, to be sure. But it's conspiracy by a thousand paper cuts. *This is too many unanswered questions*, the film shouts, quietly, at the viewer. *This many unanswered questions should bother you*.

But if you ask Dylan, he'll tell you the government-conspiracy stuff was never the point. He's actually not into conspiracies. For him, the point of making the film was to show there's too much stuff—important stuff—we still don't know about the events of 9/11. If an amateur filmmaker barely out of high school needed to be the one to catalog and present these unknowns, so be it.

But in presenting these unanswered questions, an amateur like Dylan Avery and a film like *Loose Change* inevitably raise a few more. Like, *How could those in charge never feel the need to acknowledge all the stuff they* don't *know?*

And, *Are we going to let them get away with that?*

༄ ༄ ༄

Dylan Avery was raised by two parents: a single mom and film. He and his hardworking mom spent much of their precious time together watching movies, sparking Dylan's passion for the medium at a young age. In high school, he and his best friend (and fellow "film geek"), Korey Rowe, taught themselves the basics of film production using borrowed equipment. Neither loved the academic side of school, so they spent their hours trapped on campus messing around with digital editing software, mini DVD cameras, and rudimentary forms of green screen.

When 9/11 happened, Dylan had just started his senior year of high school, and Korey, who'd graduated the previous spring, had just enlisted in the army. It was terrible timing. The towers fell, and Korey was promptly sent off to fight the fledgling wars in Afghanistan and Iraq.

Dylan stayed behind and finished his senior year, but it was a struggle. He missed making homemade movies with Korey. He also worried about his friend fighting in wars that seemed to be escalating rather than resolving anything. It was hard to understand how the wars in Afghanistan and Iraq had anything to do with fighting terrorism—their expressed purpose. The wars seemed, even to a teenager, barely related to the reason they were being fought.

After high school, Dylan applied twice to Purchase College in New York to study film. He got rejected both times. Undeterred, he decided to tend at a local bar, save up some cash, and make an independent film. He didn't, however, know what the film would be about. He spent his hours behind the bar ruminating about what story he wanted to tell.

Then, one night, none other than Tony Soprano himself—actor James Gandolfini—walked into the bar. Dylan played it cool. He let James eat and drink in peace. Then, as James was getting ready to go, Dylan introduced himself. The two had a brief conversation that Dylan remembers like this:

Dylan: "Hey, James, can I ask you a question?"
James: "Sure, kid, what's up?"
Dylan: "Is it worth it?"
James: "What do you mean?"
Dylan: "Making films. Is it worth it?"
James: "You thinking about being an actor?"
Dylan: "No, I want to be a director."
James: "Oh, okay. Well, if you want to be a successful director, you have to have something to say to the world. You have to have a message."

Dylan shook the hand of Tony Soprano—his fairy godfather—and returned to the bar. Then he knew. "I got this advice from James," he tells me, "and immediately I was like, all right, what I want to say to the world is that I'm pissed off about 9/11."

℘ ℘ ℘

So, in mid-2002, Dylan started writing a screenplay. The original screenplay was for a fictional movie: the story of three friends who discover that 9/11 was an inside job. Through researching the facts of 9/11 for the movie, Dylan grew more and more uneasy. His fact-finding mission produced more questions than answers. The laundry list of questions he accumulated, coupled with his limited budget of $2,000, compelled Dylan to turn the film from a thriller to a documentary.

To make the first version of the documentary, Dylan relied heavily on Paul Thompson's *The Terror Timeline*, a catalog of over five thousand mainstream media reports about 9/11. The *Timeline*, which existed only online at the time, purported to show inconsistencies in news-media coverage that suggested a government cover-up, or at least government foreknowledge of the attacks. Other than the *Timeline*, public information about 9/11 was hard to come by in 2002.

"We still had very little to go off of in terms of high-definition footage and documents in general," Dylan tells me. "So in those early stages it was like, 'Let's take what I feel to be some of the most effective points that the [truther] movement has—the ones that I keep seeing repeated and the ones that I see to be effective—and distill it all down into something watchable.'"

As Dylan scoured the internet for information—sifting through facts, conjecture, and pseudoscience—Korey came home from the war. He jumped right into helping Dylan make his film. Korey also came with a surprise: a mini DVD camera he'd bought off Amazon, which in 2002 had just started expanding its product catalog beyond books.

And just like that, the team was back together. Just two guys making homespun movies on their own. Altogether, Dylan and Korey spent three years—from 2002 to 2005—compiling footage, shooting scenes on their mini DVD camera, talking to independent investigators as well as people on the ground during the attacks, and gelling it all into eighty-two minutes of compelling content.

It must be said that the first version of *Loose Change* (there would ultimately be four versions) is the most paranoid; it includes some of the crazier ideas born out of the truther movement. For example, it suggests that Flight 93 might never have crashed outside Shanksville, Pennsylvania, but was instead landed at Cleveland Hopkins Airport, where all the passengers were executed.

The paranoid vibe of the first edition is a problem that Dylan himself acknowledges. He would, over the next three editions, learn from his mistakes and shift the focus from things that *could have* happened to things that definitely did happen. For example, later versions include audio from hundreds of hours of NORAD air recordings from 9/11 that Dylan and Korey obtained by filing Freedom of Information Act requests. In releasing those recordings to the public, Dylan and Korey gave many of us our first real taste of what happened in the sky that terrible day.

Loose Change: 1st Edition was released at the end of 2005 on DVD and popped up shortly afterward on torrent sites. It became an immediate viral sensation in a time, not that long ago, when it was actually really hard to go viral.

YouTube was only a couple of months old and by no means a destination site in 2005. The internet had no free platform to upload and watch peer-to-peer videos. No mainstream media outlet would touch the film with a ten-foot pole. So, *Loose Change* relied on individual people buying physical DVDs from Dylan, ripping them onto their computers, and sharing the files with other individuals.

"The first edition of *Loose Change* came out, and it was a big underground success due to DVD sales and torrent sites. But at the time, there wasn't a place where we could just upload the video and people could watch it," Dylan recalls. "Then, right around the time I'm finishing up the second edition, I'm leaving my mom's house, and this guy who's renting a room at her house stops me and says, 'Hey, man, did you know Google is gonna do a video-sharing platform?' I said, 'Yeah, I heard about that, but I don't know how many people are gonna want to sit and watch a movie on their computer.'"

Dylan laughs at himself. "Little did I know!" Then he sighs. "Now that's all people fucking do."

※ ※ ※

In 2006, Dylan uploaded *Loose Change: 2nd Edition Recut* (which omitted many of the more outrageous claims of the first edition) to Google Video and eventually to YouTube. That's when the views really started pouring in. When asked how many views *Loose Change* got in total, Dylan says it's hard to know, partially because Google Video is now defunct and because the movie always thrived on underground torrent sites. But he's sure that—bare minimum—a hundred million people saw it.

The sheer viewership commanded by Dylan's amateur documentary was unprecedented at the time. It ushered in the era we now live in—the era of people watching shit online. While mainstream media outlets forever portrayed the content of *Loose Change* as pure pseudojournalism, they could not completely discredit its influence on media itself. In August 2006, one mainstream media outlet, *Vanity Fair*, conceded that *Loose Change* "just might be the first Internet blockbuster."[1]

"I've been ingrained in the new video revolution whether I like it or not," Dylan tells me. "When I watch YouTube channels now, a lot of stuff that I see is basically *Loose Change*. It's music and voice-over with video clips and still images."

And the film's influence didn't stop at style. It also inaugurated the era of truly free content available at the click of a button. No fees, no sponsors, no product placements, no gimmicks.

"When we had information—like the NORAD air recordings—we released it for free on the internet. It was like,

'We have information, we are now releasing it to the public because the public deserves to have it,'" Dylan tells me. "There was no catch. There was no paywall, no 'Click here to donate.' It was just, 'Here's information, have it.'"

This is my life's work. Here, have it for free. It's a move only an amateur would make. And it birthed a generation of media that only an amateur could birth.

༃ ༃ ༃

The decision to make their content completely free had consequences for Dylan and Korey, personally. In 2006, at the peak of the film's popularity, the guys struck a deal with Mark Cuban's distribution company to get it shown in movie theaters. The deal would have meant substantial revenue for them—blockbuster-movie revenue. But the deal fell apart, ultimately, because Dylan refused to take down the old editions off the internet.

"The whole point of *Loose Change* was that everybody should be able to watch it," Dylan explains to me. "If it was behind any kind of paywall, it wouldn't have been successful from our point of view."

So, the movie lives on in infamy online. It did appear for brief periods of time on Netflix and on the iTunes store but was ultimately relegated to the backwaters of the internet.

Dylan seems to feel, in some ways, the same thing happened to him. He made a bigger impact on society through film—with no formal training—than most professional filmmakers will ever make. But because he did it from a metaphorical shed out in the woods, professional filmmakers still don't get it. "Professional filmmakers still say to me, 'Well, one, you made a film about a fucking what-some-would-call conspiracy theory. And two, you gave it away for free on the internet. So why would we hire you to do anything?'"

Dylan, now a decade and a half out from *Loose Change: 1st Edition*, still pursues mainstream moviemaking opportunities when they arise. When the pickings are slim, he makes films on his own. One of his recent independent documentaries, *Black and Blue*, is a gritty, hardline look at police brutality. In 2017, it won Best Documentary at the Catalina Film Festival.[2]

"Were you looking to make another quote-unquote controversial documentary?" I ask him.

"Not at all," he replies. "I struggled with making [*Black and Blue*] for a good year. I really didn't want to . . . but things just kept happening and then I had a couple run-ins with the police myself. Then I was like, 'This is just fucking ridiculous. These guys are out of control.'" He pauses. "Like *Loose Change*, I wasn't going out of my way to make a film about something controversial; it just kind of coalesced. When I'm upset—angry—about something, I need to do something about it."

I remain silent for a second, and Dylan continues.

"I'm just this little guy over here who kinda sorta knows how to make films, and that's how I express myself when I'm upset. But it would be nice to not be upset and just make films for film's sake."

༜ ༜ ༜

In talking to Dylan Avery, I get the sense that, much like Sheila Wysocki, he doesn't really *want* to be doing what he's doing. He wants to make movies—that much is clear. But I think, in any other world, Dylan would have preferred to go to film school, get a degree, and live a professional life behind a mainstream Hollywood camera.

But sometime when he was still young, he encountered the troubles of this world and became unable to shut those troubles out. He became unable to overlook the obvious oversights of people in power. He got sucked into a vacuum of power, super unprepared. And he (unqualified as all hell) tried to do some of the work that should have been done by the professionals.

Was it a brave thing to do? Or a stupid thing? It seems when you're angry enough, there's little difference.

If Sheila Wysocki was called to amateurism by a dreamlike vision, then Dylan Avery got into a head-on collision with amateurism. He felt the full impact of global fear and anger, stumbled away, and still to this day looks back with bewilderment. "I had this massive success that I wasn't prepared for when I was relatively young, and I had to spend the rest of my formative years dealing with it," he tells me. "And here I am, thirty-four years old, and sometimes I'm still like, 'Wait, what the fuck happened again?'"

The events of 9/11 are a part of Dylan's story whether he likes it or not. The same is true for America. And many Americans feel something similar to what Dylan feels: a faint undercurrent of *Wait, what the fuck happened again?*

To Dylan, the reason this feeling lingers is that the authorities betrayed us. They double-betrayed us, actually. The first betrayal was their inability to protect us. The second betrayal was their seeming lack of interest in finding out what they didn't already know. The second betrayal was, in terms of long-term healing, the worse one. As people used to say about the Watergate scandal, it's not the crime, it's the cover-up.

"I think the anger and the fear [we feel today] stems from us still not having an honest conversation about what happened on 9/11," Dylan says. "The people in power didn't even give us a real investigation. And we're trying to act like we've moved on, we've had our wars, whatever. But we're not over it. We as a nation have a certain sort of PTSD."

Amateurs can't undo a betrayal performed by an authority figure. But amateurs can spark those *more honest conversations* that we need. They can ask the taboo questions that those in the know would never ask. With no professional reputations to lose, they can do real investigations. Or at least they can try.

THE AMATEUR'S CODE OF ETHICS

A great master amateur uses his anger at an authority figure's failing to fuel an independent search for information. He releases his findings to the public to facilitate a more honest conversation between authorities and the general population. When asked what qualifies him to perform such an investigation, he says his credentials are his existence and his common sense. He will not be intimidated or put down from trying. He cannot be made to feel less than. He already knows he's an amateur, after all.

He uses his mastery of independent research to gather information and his facility with peer-to-peer communication to disseminate that information. He may offer an interpretation of that information, but he doesn't pretend to know all the answers. He knows that he does not know everything. When he cannot find a fact-based answer to a question, he allows it to remain an unanswered question. He does not scribble in an answer with face-saving conjecture.

This is indeed an important ability of the master amateur: to both seek knowledge and embrace ignorance at the same time. We try, and in trying we often find concrete answers to overlooked questions. And . . . sometimes we don't. When we don't, we freely admit that we haven't found an answer yet. We do both—seek knowledge and admit ignorance—because it keeps us honest.

※ ※ ※

And now, a word of caution. Normally, at this point in a chapter, I'd tell you to be brave, be free, be reckless. Go do that thing you don't know how to do and be proud of it. But this time, I encourage you to be prudent. When you set out to dig up buried information and distribute it, be reasonable and stick to verifiable facts. Consider your sources. Limit the scope of your investigation to specific questions. Stay focused.

I say this because, unlike professionals, we amateurs have few safeguards in place to keep us from going off the rails. We like this fact, generally. But an angry amateur with no checks or balances in place can cause havoc and become the worst of our kind: a fearmonger, proponent of hate, agent of stupidity, and straight-up shit-stirrer. We can become "fake news." We can become the conspiracy theorists who even amateur investigators despise—the ones who willfully ignore facts, science, and reason.

When I spoke to Dylan Avery, he told me these willfully ignorant amateurs are epitomized, in his mind, by the so-called flat-Earth theorists—people who believe that the authorities are lying to us about the Earth being round.

"It's one thing to have information at your disposal and to go through that information, distill it down to a conclusion, and recognize that conclusion contradicts what you've been told by authorities," Dylan told me. "It's one thing to point out factual flaws in, say, a government investigation. It's another thing to be like, 'Well, you know what? If the Earth *was* flat, NASA wouldn't want *you* to know about it.' That's, like, not a fact. That's just you being fucking paranoid."

This is, in my opinion, perhaps the greatest danger master amateurs face as a community: the possibility that we can spread paranoia and ignorance without having to account for it. So how do we not do this? The answer is, luckily, pretty simple. We live by a code of ethics.

༄ ༄ ༄

To imagine an amateur's code of ethics, I say we look at the profession that's in many ways our closest relative: journalism. Journalism, unlike law or medicine, is not a profession that requires one to have a specific degree or license to practice. It's harder—in terms of formal education and licensing—to become a professional plumber or welder than it is to become a professional journalist.

Instead of credentials, the thing that holds journalism together as a coherent discipline and gives it standing in society is its code of ethics. A professional journalist is expected to be accurate, be impartial, seek the truth, avoid conflicts of interest, hold themselves accountable, and consider the impact their words have on others. A journalist is respected by the wider community only if they adhere to these guidelines—if they maintain a track record of ethical decisions.

We, as a community, should do the same thing. I am no ethicist (not yet, anyway), but I propose our ethical standards as master amateurs should include:

- Don't lie, mislead, misrepresent, or oversimplify. (See chapter 3, "Greed.")
- Provide context. Something may be true in one context and not true in another.
- Be upfront about your personal biases and motives.
- Don't overblow your conclusions.
- Correct errors when you're wrong.
- Involve single-subject experts when their knowledge could help you.

If we follow these ethical guidelines, not only can we avoid spreading hate, fear, and nonsense, but I think we can actually be *better* disseminators of information than the professionals are. Amateurs have a lot of advantages when it comes to running investigations and sharing their findings. They're often closer to the action and more familiar with the players involved. They have a better understanding of what "regular" people care about. Amateurs also have the freedom to publish their material directly to the public without it being vetted (and possibly adulterated) by Big Media and its corporate interests.

All in all, amateurs—when they have an ethical backbone—can provide a more honest, less contrived account of real-life events. One amateur has even, just recently, exposed one of the worst public-health failings this country has ever known.

ANGER, TAPPED

In the autumn of 2014, LeeAnne Walters noticed the water that flowed from her kitchen faucet was changing colors. The colors mirrored the changing maple leaves outside her window—first yellow, then gold, then rust brown. Something was happening to LeeAnne and her family as well. Rashes dotted her twin toddlers. Her oldest daughter suffered chronic abdominal pain. Her three-year-old son, Gavin, had blurry vision that wouldn't quit. Doctors tried to pacify LeeAnne by saying he probably had cancer.

But others in LeeAnne's neighborhood on the south side of Flint, Michigan, had sudden, mysterious health problems as well. Many suspected that their water was making them sick; some residents attended city-council meetings with clumps of hair and bottles of swamp water in their hands. They knew something was wrong. But those in power—everyone from local city officials to the governor of Michigan, Rick Snyder—insisted that Flint water was safe to drink.

LeeAnne, unsatisfied with that response, demanded the city test her tap water for contaminants. They agreed and then stalled the test for three months. When the results finally came back, LeeAnne learned she and her family had been drinking water with lead levels at 104 parts per billion—seven times the legal limit. A second test said it was more like 397 parts per billion. A third test (which LeeAnne only obtained later through a Freedom of Information Act request) said it was 707 parts per billion.

In other words, Gavin did not have cancer. He had lead poisoning.

Word of LeeAnne's leaded water spread like wildfire through Flint, and city officials did all they could to contain it. They insisted the problem was isolated to LeeAnne's home. The mayor of Flint, Dayne Walling, went on local TV and flippantly drank tap water out of a white coffee mug. One city official even insinuated that LeeAnne might be spiking her own water with lead to get attention.

So LeeAnne, infuriated at the authorities' negligence, decided to prove that the whole town's water was poisoned herself.

༄ ༄ ༄

First she recruited a regional EPA manager to help her obtain technical documents about Flint's water system. Through those documents, she learned that just a few months earlier, in the throes of a budget crisis, city officials had switched Flint's municipal water source from Lake Huron to the Flint River. They did it to save $5 million in utility costs over the next two years. The Flint River was a former industrial dumping zone and was known to have corrosive water that leached lead and other metals off pipes unless it was treated with an anticorrosive agent. But LeeAnne, to her dismay, could find no evidence that the water ever was treated with an anticorrosive agent.

This was almost certainly the source of the city's sudden sickness. But now she had to prove it with science. "We decided to get to the science of it," she later told a reporter, "because you can't argue with science."[3]

To get to the science of it, LeeAnne contacted Marc Edwards, a professor of civil and environmental engineering at Virginia Tech. Marc and his lab had exposed a similar lead crisis in Washington, DC, a decade earlier. LeeAnne told Marc that her goal was to get all of Flint's water tested independently of the government, and that she would like his lab to help. He immediately agreed.

Marc sent LeeAnne a supply of tamperproof plastic bottles with which to gather water samples. He said they would need at least seventy-five samples to show a pattern of contamination. LeeAnne took the bottles and walked the streets of Flint, systematically drawing samples from each zip code. She ensured every sample had a clear chain of custody back to Marc's lab. She also recruited her neighbors to scale up the effort. One of those neighbors, Keri Webber, would later say, "LeeAnne was amazing at keeping everybody headed the right direction, keeping everything scientifically correct so we could get the answers we had to have."[4]

Within three weeks, LeeAnne and her team had sent Marc's lab over eight hundred samples to test.

The results of the tests showed that one in six homes in Flint had water with lead levels above EPA safety standards. This meant that around one hundred thousand people had been exposed to unsafe levels of lead. Many of those people had full-blown lead poisoning, the effects of which never go away. The neighborhoods with the highest levels of lead in their water also happened to be the poorest ones.

Authorities could not reasonably deny this evidence, but remediation to the public was far from swift. In March 2015—a year after it had switched to Flint River water—the city voted to turn the taps back. However, a special manager appointed by the state to deal with Flint's financial crisis overruled the vote. It wasn't until January 2016, when President Obama declared a state of emergency in Flint, that Michigan officials admitted their failings and started to take steps to safeguard Flint's water.

To date, the state of Michigan has spent $240 million trying to fix the problem it caused in Flint, and fifteen government officials have been indicted for contributing to, or covering up, the water crime of the century.

℘ ℘ ℘

Today—a short five years since her tap ran brown—LeeAnne Walters is a full-time public-health advocate and environmental activist. She travels the country teaching individuals in local communities how to run water-safety tests on their own. She has obtained a US Water Study grant to expand her efforts and has testified before Congress, demanding they close the loopholes in federal law that made the Flint water crisis possible.

"I'm a citizen scientist now . . . ," she told *Fast Company*, "trying to teach people to take water into their own hands, because they have a right to protect themselves."[5]

In 2018, LeeAnne won a Goldman Environmental Prize, an award that recognizes the most impactful grassroots environmentalists across the world. In her acceptance speech, she showed the steely defiance for which she's become known. "The people in charge didn't believe us when we spoke out, and there were many attempts to discredit us," she said. "But . . . we were able to prove the facts of what had happened. We finally had science on our side and the proof that couldn't be dismissed."[6]

And then, reflecting on the advice she would give her kids in the future, she simply said, "When someone tells you to stop, ignore them."[7]

Erin Brockovich, the famous amateur environmental activist who revealed that PG&E was poisoning the people of Hinkley, California, back in 1993, thinks LeeAnne is courageous but hardly alone in this world. She's part of a diffuse yet indomitable army of amateur activists. "I've been doing this for 20 years," Brockovich said, "and in every community there is a LeeAnne, and they're pissed . . . They're told, 'You're not a doctor or a scientist or a lawyer, you have no business getting involved in this.' But they will not take no for an answer."[8]

We can look at LeeAnne's story in two ways. It holds within it two truths. First, it's tragic that she had to become a citizen scientist and amateur investigator under these circumstances. It should never have happened, and one could argue that she had no choice in the matter.

But, of course, she did have a choice—the choice to either take "Shut up" for an answer or to tap into her anger and launch an investigation on her own. LeeAnne chose the latter, and in that choice she revealed the second truth: that professional public servants sometimes fail, and when they do—when they open a fire hydrant of wrongdoing onto a community—it's a triumph for an amateur to force the hydrant closed with facts.

AN ARMY OF AMATEUR ACTIVISTS

At the beginning of this book, I said that we master amateurs are a community; we just don't know it yet. That's never truer than when it comes to activism. We are all amateur activists with untapped anger about something. If we work together as a community, we have a much better chance to change the things that most outrage us. As American anthropologist

Margaret Mead once said: "Never doubt that a small group of thoughtful, committed citizens can change the world; indeed, it's the only thing that ever has."[9]

Even better, we are a *large* group of thoughtful, committed citizens.

Our large community can amplify any one individual's discovery. We can spread the word, compare notes, and make introductions. We can help each other, encourage each other, and teach each other. We should also check each other. Like any community with standards, we should hold each other accountable. That doesn't mean belittling each other as unfit simply for being an amateur (as the professionals would). It means reminding each other of our ethical standards.

Be truthful. Be transparent about your motives. Provide context. Enlist an expert when you need expertise. Admit when you're ignorant or wrong. Don't go around scaring people because you found something scary. Just tell them what you found.

And remember, the code of ethics I've outlined in this chapter is just a starting point. I now give it over to you, the perfectly capable master amateurs, to refine and remember.

When you need an example to reference, think of LeeAnne Walters. No one in this world had more right to be furious at an authority's failing. The authorities literally poisoned her kids. No one would have blamed her if she'd flown completely off the handle.

And yet she controlled herself enough to be methodical and do her investigation right—the way it needed to be done to be effective. She limited the scope of her accusations to things she could prove or disprove. She focused on proving her points using science, not conjecture. She involved government agents and professionals when they could help her. And now she teaches others, with cool resolve, tangible tactics to find facts for themselves.

So, fire yourself up and then cool yourself down. Take your anger and apply it, properly. And remember the words of peace activist Scilla Elworthy: "Anger is like gasoline, and if you spray it around and somebody lights a match, you've got an inferno. But . . . if we can put our anger inside an engine, it can drive us forward."[10]

CHAPTER 8
PERSONALITY

Be yourself. Everyone else is already taken.
—Oscar Wilde

THE BUSINESS OF FRIENDSHIP

Dear reader. Please. Do me a solid. Stop reading this book right now and go Google the name Ali Spagnola. Just kidding. Don't stop reading this book. *Ever.* Just kidding again. Actually, don't Google Ali Spagnola. Now all you want to do is Google her, right? Because I told you not to? That's so *you. Don't think about pirates. Aaarrrggghh* you thinking about pirates?
(˚ ᴗ ˚)
Well. *Don't* stay right here and let me tell you about Ali.

Ali Spagnola is a number of things. She's a musician who's produced four albums independently of any record label. She's a self-described "one-gal band" who performs multiple instruments live—drums, keys, guitar, saxophone, etc.—all at the same time. She's a sketch comedian and all-around humorist. She's a painter who, to date, has given away twenty-seven hundred paintings to anyone who asks, for free. She's an amateur Olympic weight lifter who is—as the meatheads say—"jacked." She's a former competitive ice-skater, former graphic designer, former ringtone composer, former aspiring normal person, and present-day social media influencer.

And although you've probably never heard of her, Ali is bona fide *internet famous*.

She's got over three million followers across the "Big Four" social networks: Twitter, YouTube, Instagram, and Facebook. On the smaller networks, she's also well known. When Snapchat first became a thing, Ali started a schtick called "Snapchat stunts" and became one of the app's biggest draws. When Vine was alive, she was one of its six-second superstars (RIP Vine 🙏). Today, she's helping popularize an up-and-coming social network called Twitch by livestreaming her iron-pumping workouts exclusively on the platform.

Over the course of her five-year ~*influencer*~ career, Ali has engaged her audience by performing twenty-six dance crazes hands-free on a bicycle. She has set the Guinness World Record for the fastest hundred-meter dash on a space hopper. She has refined to perfection the "beer mile"—a mile-long run where she stops every quarter mile to chug a beer. She's installed a swimming pool of water beads in her living room and dived right in.

Despite all appearances, Ali's not doing this stupid shit for fun. Well, she is doing it for fun. But fun is just the beginning. She's also doing it for work. Her vaudevillian internet performances are how she pays the bills. Through sponsorship platform Patreon, Ali gets paid directly by her audience to produce her personal brand of content: positive vibes for a nonsensical world. And she works hard, producing said content (which regularly includes cover songs, workout hacks, and observational comedy routines) at a biweekly clip.

If I wanted to, I could end Ali's story right here. She easily qualifies as a master amateur by way of her alternative vocation and her embrace of the omni-career. In the tradition of Charu Sharma, she does a little bit of everything without concern for doing any of it especially well. She embodies the amateur ethos that work and play need not be mutually exclusive. When I spoke to her, she said just about the most master-amateurish thing I've heard to date: "I don't have any hobbies," she said, "because technically a hobby is something you do and you don't get paid for it. Everything I do, I just turn into this social media thing that I do, and then suddenly that becomes my income. So, I've yet to *not* do anything professionally."

So, Ali demonstrates for us how to have hobbies for a living. Do what's fun for you, and the money will follow. But like I said earlier, fun is just the beginning. Work for fun is not the only lesson Ali has to teach us. It's not even the main lesson.

The main lesson starts with a sad truth: people today are fucking lonely. An incredible *half* of Americans consider themselves lonely, and the youngest generation (those born between the mid-1990s and the early 2000s) are the loneliest.[1] Young, lonely people are drawn to social media to try to alleviate their loneliness—to try to find a human connection.

And there they meet Ali. Musician. Comedian. Fitness inspiration. Beer lover. Above all, a new internet best friend.

Back in 2014, a local news outlet interviewed Ali in her hometown of Pittsburgh, Pennsylvania. The reporter conducting the interview needed a sound bite to summarize what this thing—this "social media thing"—is that Ali's doing with her life. With a raspy chuckle, Ali offered this: "I am cultivating a meaningful relationship with millions of people."[2]

In keeping with her brand, that's a stupid joke. And it's also not.

༄ ༄ ༄

Ali's ~*best friend*~ career began in college at Carnegie Mellon University, where, in addition to earning a degree in art, she got deep into the live-music scene. Her girl-with-a-guitar gigs, however, lacked a certain something. They lacked, she would come to decide, the kind of instant camaraderie that comes only from communal binge drinking.

"I was playing a regular live show where I was just a musician, like, strumming a guitar and I was like, 'This is boring, and I don't even want to invite people to this because, *ugh*, it's music they've never heard from an artist they don't know,'" she explains. "At the same time, I was also throwing parties in college. And I realized I'd rather invite someone to a party. So, I turned my concert into a party."

Ali composed sixty original songs to perform as a live-music set slash drinking game. Each song was one minute long, and each time Ali transitioned from one song to the next, members of the audience would take a shot of beer. This became known as her Power Hour—an interactive drinking game mashed up with a live-music concert. It was a hit. "Everybody was like best friends at the end [of the show] because we all got drunk together," she recalls. "And suddenly there were lines around the block to get in to my shows."

Like Dionysus, the god of wine and good cheer, Ali made friends out of strangers. She brought people together for a night to remember. Or forget!

Ali performed her Power Hour throughout her college years, and after graduation, she toured the country performing it at clubs and bars. She also released the sixty-song set on a USB drive stored, appropriately enough, inside a shot glass.

But after about a year of touring, Ali started to hear the reverberations of society telling her to get a real job. She decided to hang up her shot glass and join the real world. She got a real job as a graphic designer for a real company, and just a few months later that real company went out of business.

So, like a true master amateur, Ali moved on to the next thing. She was neither shocked nor devastated when she lost this "real" job. She was kind of grateful. In many ways, she'd had better job stability when she was just doing her own thing. Now that a career restart was forced upon her, she decided to go back into the business of fun. "I had known that I wanted to step in that direction [of making social media content] anyway," she says, "so it was really helpful that my job just sort of disappeared from underneath me."

In 2015, Ali moved from Pittsburgh to LA to pursue a career as an "internet creator"—the digital era's version of a small-town girl moving to Hollywood to become a star. She set herself the goal of posting one original video to social media every Thursday, and since then, she's never missed a Thursday.

To her credit, Ali racked up followers quickly. Her wit, athleticism, and willingness to look foolish made her that right balance of approachable and aspirational. When she didn't know how to do something, she'd just try anyway and show her followers the process. Her penchant for living in sports bras and biker shorts didn't hurt either. (When I ask her how she transitioned from making mostly comedy content to fitness content, she says, "I just stopped wearing shirts!")

But while she was steadily building an audience, Ali was having a low-key identity crisis. She could not easily explain what she was doing—to others, but perhaps more importantly, to herself. In the back of her mind, questions lingered. *Who should I be? What should I be focusing on? It's great that people like my content . . . but why do they like it?*

She was having the kind of existential crisis that's annoying, to start. *Who am I? What should I do?* But it's a crisis that also creates practical problems. If you don't know what your audience wants from you, how can you consistently give them what they want? If you don't know what content your audience prefers, how do you decide where to spend your time and resources? These are not ~social media~ questions; they're business questions. They're questions that need to be answered if you want to build a sustainable business.

So, Ali got her audience to answer those questions. And the answer was... ¯_(ツ)_/¯.

We don't really care, her audience answered. *We just like being with you.*

As she describes it, "I would continuously ask my audience, like, 'Hey, do you want to see more comedy sketches?' And they'd be like, 'Yeah, that's awesome!' And then I'd ask them, 'Do you want to hear more diet tips?' And they'd be like, 'Yeah, we love that!' For a while, I couldn't figure it out. What content did they really want from me?" She pauses. "Then I realized they're just there to hang out with me."

As it turned out, the content of her social media content was semi-irrelevant. Ali's audience was there for *her*. Once she realized this, she reflected this shift in thinking by telling *Forbes* magazine in 2018, "The one thing my audience knows they're getting when they come to my channel is my personality."[3]

In other words, Ali could give her audience a rudimentary saxophone lesson or show them the right way to microwave chicken or tell them the story of that time she asked a cop to hold her beer. If a follower learned something, or got inspired to do something, or had a laugh, that was great. But it wasn't really the point. The point was to enjoy Ali's company.

That's because Ali isn't in the business of *what*, like so many others are. She's in the business of *who*.

❧ ❧ ❧

Of all the master amateurs I've profiled in this book, I suspect professionals would deride Ali Spagnola the most. She's the kind of amateur who infuriates certain people—the kind who just puts a bunch of shit up online and calls it work.

I'd argue, however, that Ali is actually seizing one of the biggest entrepreneurial opportunities of our time: the ability of regular people to create *personal brands*. Personal brands are not based on the creator's expertise in anything in particular. They're based on her likability. They're based on her ability to form connections with many people all at once. They're brands—businesses—that are, quite literally, *personal*.

And social media is, for many proprietors of a personal brand, the best place to start. It's the best place to reach masses of people in an unfiltered fashion. Once they've gotten some attention, the proprietor might sell their audience tangible products, like Matt Monahan does with his Instagram followers. Or they might accept financial support from their audience, like Ali does using Patreon, turning each fan into a micro-Medici.

Either way, their business is fundamentally *not* about products. It's about people.

And despite what professionals might think, it *is* work. It's not the work we've prized for the last century—the diligent mastering of a single subject. It's a different kind of work. It's the work of *putting yourself out there*. To be liked by people on a large scale, one must be diligently genuine, honest, endearing, and *real*. Vulnerable, even. In front of millions of strangers, no less.

This is, in many ways, the quintessential master amateur's endeavor: to live and thrive and gain the support of others by exposing one's quirks, insecurities, ineptitudes, and flights of fancy. Not to mention one's face, voice, and—usually—apartment. These master amateurs show us that, in this world, you can succeed by being great. But you can also succeed by being *yourself*.

When I speak to Ali, I ask her if she ever struggles with putting herself out there in front of so many people. Specifically, I ask her if she ever feels insecure.

"You mean, like, how many times a day?" she quips. "Yes, absolutely. I think if you don't feel insecure, you're just not thinking very hard. Tina Fey talks about this [in her autobiography, *Bossypants*]. She talks about one second feeling like, 'I'm a genius! This is great! Everyone bow down to me.' And then the next second feeling like, 'Oh my God, I'm so embarrassed and stupid and wrong.' So yeah, it's a wide range of emotions."

So, it is work. It's emotional work. And to our collective parents' dismay, it's a type of work that young people are increasingly aspiring to do. In a 2017 survey of one thousand kids aged six to seventeen, over 50 percent said they wanted to be a social media creator (specifically a YouTuber) when they grew up.[4] I ask Ali what advice she'd give those kids. Without hesitation, she says, "Figure out what's fun for you, and make that. Do that. *Follow your fun.* Don't try to reverse engineer what you think people want from you."

Today, Ali embraces her career as an internet best friend. She calls her followers her "pal-y community" and starts every video by cheering, "Hey, best pal-y, I'm Ali!" She then proceeds to show them her new pair of mismatched shoes, or explain why she's eating more fat these days, or whatever. It hardly matters. They're just three million friends hanging out together on the internet's living room sofa. They could talk about anything or nothing. That's the way it is when you just like being together.

LIKE-ABILITY

Great master amateurs connect with wide swaths of people by being authentically themselves. They build personal brands—brands that are *personal*—by being honest, transparent, funny, stupid, and real. They incorporate their true personalities into their work and in the process form human connections on a large scale. These connections, if cultivated, become communities of supporters that help drive a master amateur's career forward. Within these communities lies a master amateur's opportunity to make a living and thrive.

At the end of the day, these master amateurs have no qualifications to do anything. People just like them.

But don't be fooled into thinking that's an accident. Some individuals are naturally charming, to be sure, but these master amateurs purposefully enhance their likability. How? By doing the emotional work of being openly themselves, including the unflattering bits. Why? Because their openness—particularly the unflattering bits—draws to them an invaluable resource: an invested and supportive audience.

Now, a quick digression. I think many people see something negative in the rise of personal brands. It's easy to criticize personal brands as being too pedestrian or too narcissistic or perhaps even sinister—to see them as a way for one person to gain financially off other people's desire for connection.

Here are my thoughts. Are they pedestrian? Yes, definitely. Anyone can develop a personal brand. That's exactly why they are a huge entrepreneurial opportunity. Are they narcissistic? They can be. If the proprietor of a personal brand chooses to sell his audience apparel with his face on it and that's it, then sure, it's pretty narcissistic.

Are they sinister? I don't think so. I see personal brands—specifically the kinds that have grown up on social media—as attempts to revive something we've lost. That is, the casual gathering place. Just a few decades ago, people would gather around a local establishment like a pub or a beauty parlor for some low-key socializing. They'd pay the proprietor of the establishment a small fee to be there; they'd buy some drinks or get their hair done. But really, they were there to chat, gossip, and *be with others* in a low-pressure environment.

Those types of environments don't readily exist anymore. At least not IRL. So, personality-based social media channels are moving in to fill some of the void. They are places where people can gather and chat and listen to stories and hang out. Occasionally, the host will ask his patrons to purchase something so the place can stay in business. That's really it. It's a watering hole for the socially thirsty.

Let me give you an example. First, you must know something about me: I love true-crime stories. Or as my husband likes to say, ~*I love murder*~. For most of my life, this was a poorly hidden secret. I'd sneak into the basement of my childhood home late at night to watch *Unsolved Mysteries* or *Forensic Files*, hoping no one would discover me and think me a creep. I was only slightly less ashamed of my love of murder as an adult. Then, on a fateful day in 2016, a certain podcast caught my eye as I scrolled the iTunes store. Its name was . . . *My Favorite Murder*.

Other people have favorite murders?! I thought. For so long I believed myself to be the only one.

My Favorite Murder is a podcast hosted by two IRL friends: Karen Kilgariff and Georgia Hardstark. In each episode, Karen tells Georgia one true-crime story, and Georgia tells Karen another. Neither of them has any professional background in criminal investigation, forensics, justice, or anything like that. Georgia is the host of a show on the Cooking Channel, and Karen is a comedy writer.

Just to make it even more amateurish, the two of them spend a great deal of each episode talking about their lives. They go on long digressions about their childhoods, their vacation plans, their outfits, their triumphs, and their anxieties. They use an unprofessional amount of swear words. Karen talks openly about how she used to be a drunk (and sometimes does a "Drunk Karen" voice). Georgia tells us more than we ever needed to know about her cats.

In other words, they're just regular people discussing a topic as any regular people would: poorly, but delightfully. And these ramblings—this *filler*—is why we, the audience, listen each week. We came for the crime, but we've stayed for the charm.

And, it turns out, a lot of people like listening to two charming ladies talk about crime plus whatever. According to iTunes, *My Favorite Murder* gets up to nineteen million downloads per month.[5] In just three years, Karen and Georgia have earned millions of social media followers, a book deal, their own podcast network, and a loyal community of fans who call themselves Murderinos. Karen and Georgia produce *My Favorite Murder* merchandise that the Murderino community happily buys up. They also sell their community tickets to live performances all around the world. On Halloween 2018, they sold out the seven-thousand-seat Microsoft Theater in Los Angeles, making *My Favorite Murder* the bestselling live podcast show of all time.

So, Karen and Georgia have benefited from being themselves sans qualifications. And the Murderinos—the closeted crime lovers who've finally found each other—are developing friendships that go well beyond telling each other scary stories. They connect online, support each other, share their deepest fears, and occasionally meet up in real life. Two amateurs walk away with a profitable business, and untold numbers of strangers are strangers no longer.

༄ ༄ ༄

In the same way IRL watering holes were good business in their time, social media channels slash personal brands are good business today. In some ways, they're better business because, while they still capitalize on people's desire for connection, they're much less susceptible to shifting external factors than traditional businesses are.

For example, a personal brand won't go out of business because of a downturn in the economy, like a brick-and-mortar establishment might. A personal brand won't be laid to waste by a new technology, like many skill-based businesses have been. A personal brand won't become public domain, like much knowledge work has—making those knowledge-based businesses obsolete.

We know that skills and knowledge are moving farther and farther away from individual people. The skill of driving is shifting away from the driver and into the car. The skill of photography is shifting away from the photographer and into the camera. The knowledge of the travel agent, for instance, has already shifted completely into the travel website.

The one thing that's *not* moving farther away from the individual is the individual himself. The one thing that isn't shifting away from you is *you*. A new technology may be able to do what you do, but it cannot *be* who you *are*.

This is what the creators of personal brands are trumpeting. It may be narcissistic. It may be base. Nevertheless, the creators of personal brands are a rebellious horde, running across the metaphorical highlands of Scotland, yelling, *You may take our lives, but you'll never take our personalities!!!!!!1!!11*

Here's the kicker. This great new, future-resistant entrepreneurial opportunity—the personal brand—is squarely in the wheelhouse of the amateur. Why? Because you cannot go to school to learn how to be yourself. You cannot take a test to see if you're ready to be *real* or not. Professional schooling is about learning content, and if, as in Ali's case, the content of your brand is semi-irrelevant, then the professional route is irrelevant too. It will teach you *what*, and sometimes *how*. But never *who*.

Only you know who you are.

So, those who choose the path of the personal brand are *obligate amateurs*. They have to learn the skills of amateurism to succeed. There is no other way. There's no professional path that can teach them what they need to know, which is, above all, how to connect mentally and emotionally with others. Even if a college someday decided to offer a likability course, it wouldn't work. Those who graduated from it would be too self-conscious; they would appear contrived, and being contrived is the opposite of what makes personal brands work.

In many of the other disciplines I've discussed in this book, being an amateur is an option. Forrest Mims could have been a professional or an amateur climate scientist. Dylan Avery could have been a professional or an amateur documentarian. But Ali Spagnola could not have been a professional or an amateur social media influencer. There is no meaningful distinction between the two. She's a professional social media influencer because she makes a living at it. She's more so an amateur social media influencer because she has no training or qualifications to do what she's doing. She's just making it all up as she goes along.

This is how more and more careers will be. They will be less skill based, less knowledge based, and more personality based. As a result, they will draw less distinction between *amateur* and *professional*, and the skills of the amateur will be as important, if not more important, than the skills of the professional.

In the emerging likability industry, there are not two roads that diverged in a wood. There is only one: the foot-trod path of the master amateur. And like Ali, someday soon, lots of people will confidently say they've never *not* done anything professionally.

YOU CAN'T TAKE CLASSES TO LEARN HOW TO BE WONDERFUL

On February 11, 1962, an unknown American chef named Julia Child appeared on Boston public television to discuss her debut cookbook, *Mastering the Art of French Cooking*. The host, Albert Duhamel, flipped the pages of the massive, 726-page book, preparing to ask his guest some softball questions about French cooking. Then Julia suddenly stood up, revealing her *grande* six-foot-two-inch frame. She pulled out the hot plate she'd brought with her and plugged it into the wall. She cracked some eggs into a bowl. As she vigorously whisked and folded the eggs, she answered Albert's questions about French cooking in the warbly voice for which she would become known. She prepared on air that day an *omelette gratinée aux champignons* (an omelette with mushroom sauce). Soon after, the TV station received an unprecedented twenty-seven letters asking for more cooking demonstrations à la Julia.

That day in 1962, Julia Child—without knowing it—launched her career as America's first celebrity chef. She was fifty years old. Over the second half of her life, she'd produce dozens of TV shows and cookbooks that'd earn her a Peabody Award, a National Book Award, the Presidential Medal of Freedom, the French Legion of Honor, the first-ever Emmy Award for an educational TV show, a permanent display in the Smithsonian National Museum of American History, and ten honorary doctorates.

Julia Child was not the first person to cook on TV, but she was the first to use the medium to dramatically change the way Americans ate at home. Before Julia, TV dinners reigned supreme. People thought a tuna casserole *avec le* Jell-O was an accomplished meal. French food (and all "foreign" food, really) was relegated to the restaurant, and that restaurant had snobby, mustachioed waiters judging one's pronunciation.

Julia would have none of that. She would not let Americans suffer gross food because they felt intimidated. So, she made herself into the least intimidating French chef they knew. During the ten-year run of her first show, *The French Chef*, Julia insisted that all episodes be aired unedited so viewers could see the mistakes she made while cooking. And she made *a lot* of mistakes. Hardly an episode passed without her splashing wine on the counters or flinging a giblet across the room. Mistakes were so much a part of Julia's personal brand that, in 1978, Dan Aykroyd parodied her on *Saturday Night Live* by cutting his finger off while deboning a chicken. As the blood spurted out, he cheerily screeched, "Accidents *do* happen in the kitchen!"

By turning down the heat on French cooking, Julia made it accessible to her audience—an audience composed primarily of American housewives who felt increasingly uncertain about their place in the world. When the women at home felt downtrodden and isolated, Julia was there to make their lives lighter and sweeter. *Butter! Cream! Sugar!* And, sprinkled in like salt, words of encouragement. "The only real stumbling block is fear of failure," Julia once declared. "In cooking you've got to have a what-the-hell attitude."[6] And, more pragmatically: "Always remember: if you're alone in the kitchen and you drop the lamb, you can always just pick it up. Who's going to know?"[7]

༡ ༡ ༡

Julia Child was well into middle age when she became a TV star. So, before she was Julia Child, she was many other things. She was an advertising copywriter for a furniture department in New York City. She was a typist for the Office of Strategic Services (the OSS) in Washington, DC, but only after being told she was too tall to enlist in the Women's Army Corps. Once in the OSS, she climbed the ranks to become a top-secret researcher (a.k.a. a spy). And when she learned that curious sharks detonated many of the underwater explosives meant to blow up German U-boats, she cooked up a clever recipe for shark repellent.

It was during her time in the OSS that Julia met her husband, Paul Child. She'd later call him her "porter, dishwasher, official photographer, mushroom dicer and onion chopper, editor, fish illustrator, manager, taster, idea man, resident poet, and husband."[8] Sounds like he was a master amateur too. In 1948, the two of them followed his career to France. Julia loved France from day one. She described her first meal in the city of Rouen (a meal of oysters, sole meunière, and fine wine) as a revelatory experience—one that inspired her to finally learn to cook. "Up until then," she liked to quip, "I just ate."[9]

In 1949, Julia enrolled at Le Cordon Bleu culinary school in Paris, having no previous experience with cooking. She was not a natural. The school deemed her "unqualified for the expert class," and she failed the graduation exam the first time she took it.[10] Nevertheless, nothing would cool her simmering passion for *beurre* and *fromage* and *oeufs*. "Until I discovered cooking," she once said, "I was never really interested in anything."[11]

Eventually, Julia did graduate from Le Cordon Bleu and began teaching American expats in Paris. Through teaching, she met Simone Beck and Louisette Bertholle, two Frenchwomen who were attempting to write the first comprehensive French cookbook in English. But their cookbook was floundering. Although it was written in English, publishers said it wasn't written *in English*. Meaning the content wasn't relatable to anyone who wasn't French.

Then Simone and Louisette met Julia. They knew from the get-go that this big, loud American woman was the perfect third coauthor—the one who could make a French cookbook palatable to English speakers. Julia agreed, and the book they produced became *Mastering the Art of French Cooking*. It would go on to become a perennial bestseller, having sold one and a half million copies to date, and it would land Julia that fateful shot at stardom on Boston public television back in February 1962.

༄ ༄ ༄

Unlike many of the master amateurs I've profiled in this book, Julia Child did not invent anything new. She was decidedly *not* innovative. She didn't have original ideas in the way that, say, Frank Lloyd Wright did. French cooking existed for decades, if not centuries, in the state that Julia learned it and taught it, and she did not add much to the craft in terms of creativity.

What she did instead was make it accessible to a new audience—*her* audience.

Julia's gift was knowing who her audience was and how to make something they considered inaccessible work for them. She understood *her people* and spoke to them directly. To the midcentury American housewives who adored her, there was no French cooking other than the French cooking narrated to them through the charming vocal fry of Julia Child.

"I think you have to decide who your audience is," Julia once advised. "If you don't pick your audience, you're lost because you're not really talking to anybody. My audience is people who like to cook, who want to really learn how to do it."[12]

That seems true, but it also seems incomplete. Julia's audience liked to cook and wanted to learn how to do it. But they also wanted to be uplifted. They wanted a connection. They came for the *boeuf* and stayed for the moral support. As one Julia superfan remembers: "There were times, as a desperate young mother living in a provincial town, when I felt that all that stood between me and insanity was hearty Julia Child."[13]

Julie Powell, author of the bestselling memoir *Julie and Julia: My Year of Cooking Dangerously*, has her thoughts on why Julia's audience felt so emotionally attached to her. "Something came out in Julia on television," she once said. "Her voice and her attitude and her playfulness. It was just magical. You can't fake that. You can't take classes to learn how to be wonderful."[14]

In other words, Julia taught her fans how to cook, but more importantly she taught them how to be authentic. She taught them how to not be intimidated. Cooking was the hook; Julia's what-the-hell attitude was the life changer. If her fans had just wanted to learn to cook, they could have taken classes, as Julia herself did. But they didn't—they watched Julia Child on TV for four solid decades. Why? Because you can't take classes to learn how to be wonderful.

CRACK OPEN THE ECHO CHAMBER

The way to develop a successful personal brand as a master amateur is, first, to understand that some things are teachable and some things are not. Information can be taught. Content can be taught. Techniques can be taught. As I said earlier in this chapter, the professional path will teach you *what*, and sometimes *how*, but never *who*. That's because authenticity cannot be taught. Personality cannot. These qualities spring naturally from the person who's unattached to their appearance. And who's more unattached to their appearance than a brazen amateur?

Of the master amateurs who've created their own personal brands, the most successful ones struck a beautiful balance between those things that can be taught and those things that cannot. Julia Child, for example, knew how to cook well enough to demonstrate her recipes accurately, but not *so well* that it erased her humanity. She had some substance, but not so much that it grounded her personal style. She was professional enough to communicate French cooking techniques, but amateurish enough to understand what non-cooks cared about.

Like Ali Spagnola, the hosts of *My Favorite Murder*, and Charu Sharma, Julia Child was that perfect balance of *good enough* but decidedly *not perfect*.

If she'd been any more perfect (meaning any more entrenched in the culinary profession), no one except her fellow chefs would've understood what she was talking about. Only her fellow experts would've related to the content she produced. And as so often happens, the professional echo chamber would've kept reverberating. Full of sound and fury. Signifying nothing.

Instead, Julia led with her amateurism, and in doing so she made a crack in the culinary profession's echo chamber. You can do this too. But remember, lead with your amateurism. Knowing some content is good; having some vetted techniques under your belt is helpful. But it's your amateurism—your imperfection, your humanity—that'll make relatable all the valuable content that's so often reserved for professionals only.

Now, you may wonder, how do you choose which echo chamber you want to breach? I'd take Ali's advice and "follow your fun." Pick a subject you genuinely enjoy, like food or fitness or forensics, make it your own, and allow others to enjoy it with you. Learn enough about it to have something to say. Then forget everything and just be yourself.

CHAPTER 9

LOVE

> *Work is love made visible.*
> —Khalil Gibran

MY NEW, GREATER LOVE

On a chilly evening in the summer of 1993, Harvard-educated lawyer Ben Schatz and four of his male friends attended a Bette Midler concert. For the event, the men dressed up as the Andrews Sisters—a 1940s close-harmony singing group best remembered for performing the swing ditty "Boogie Woogie Bugle Boy." Ben and his friends polished their finger waves and cinched their pencil skirts tight, assuming many other concertgoers would be in drag. This was San Francisco, after all. And it was Bette Midler.

When they arrived to find themselves the only ones in drag, all the attention fell on them. In a good way. The crowd *loved* their getups. One concertgoer (who also happened to be an event promoter) asked the guys if they could sing at her upcoming fiftieth birthday party. "We don't sing," they replied in unison. But then Ben mentioned he *did* have some musical-theater experience. So did his friends. Realizing they could *probably* sing, the five men went back to Ben's apartment and practiced three-part harmonies until three in the morning.

That night, Ben and his friends unofficially formed the Kinsey Sicks, America's Favorite Dragapella® Beautyshop Quartet (a.k.a. the premier theatrical group of men singing a cappella in drag). Since 1993, the group has produced nine albums of politically charged, satirically biting a cappella music, toured internationally, and performed at some of the most famous venues in the country, including New York's Studio 54. The men named their group the Kinsey Sicks in honor of the scale of sexuality developed by Alfred Kinsey in 1948, in which zero is completely heterosexual and six is completely homosexual.

For the last twenty-five years, Ben Schatz has performed in the Kinsey Sicks as "Rachel," a sexy minx with a loud mouth, bulging biceps, and poorly applied blush. Rachel is a feminist who does not try to look pretty; she tries to look ridiculous. The original group lineup also included Irwin Keller as "Winnie," Maurice Kelly as "Trixie," Jerry Friedman as "Vaselina," and Abatto Avilez as the sweet-smelling "Begoña."

When the men formed the group, they were, as they put it, "refugees from successful careers as professionals."[1] As a troupe of singing queens, these consummate professionals found a way to say what they really wanted to say. Or, *sing* what they wanted to say. They could be vulgar, taboo, adorable, and just a touch too honest. They could be irrepressible, unrespectable, *unprofessional.* They could be themselves. And, it turned out, they *could* sing!

At the time, Ben Schatz—"Rachel"—needed something to sing about. Since graduating from Harvard Law School eight years earlier, he'd worked full-time as a civil-rights lawyer handling HIV and AIDS discrimination cases. He had, for a period of time in the 1980s, been the *only* US attorney working full-time on HIV-related impact litigation. In 1990, Ben became the executive director of the Gay and Lesbian Medical Association. In 1992, he authored then candidate Bill Clinton's policy on HIV, and when Clinton won the election, he appointed Ben to the Presidential Advisory Council on HIV/AIDS.

The work was grueling; the fight was personal. Since the '80s, Ben had lived and worked in the Castro district of San Francisco—the gay nexus of the world and the epicenter of the AIDS epidemic. According to the Centers for Disease Control, as of October 31, 1995, over five hundred thousand people in the US had been diagnosed with HIV or AIDS. Eighty-five percent of them were men. The overwhelming majority of those men were gay. And 62 percent of them had already died.[2]

A sickening number of his friends had already died when Ben started singing. Abatto Avilez, a founding member of the Kinsey Sicks, died after just a few performances with the group. He was never replaced. So, Ben had a dubious distinction at the time; he experienced something exceedingly odd for a modern person to experience. He was roughly thirty years old, and people were dying all around him.

So, in an attempt to get society to give a shit about gay men, Ben put on his (as he puts it) "lawyer drag" and went to work. He worked hard and felt proud of the work that he did. But at the same time, Rachel constantly nagged him. She whispered in his ear, *Do me.* She haunted him, like a bratty ghost. For seven years, Ben placated her by lawyering in the day and letting her loose at night. Eventually, though, he felt it necessary to give up his hard-earned profession for his absolutely ridiculous hobby. The voice was just too strong.

I first learned of Ben's story from an article he wrote in 2000, right after he left law for good. It was published by Salon under the title "Save your Life: Sing in Drag." In it, Ben wrote, "So why did I make the final switch? Because the contrast between the joy Rachel gave and received as a performer and the stress Ben gave and received at work became too glaring to ignore."[3]

This is where Ben and I start our conversation: not in career number one or in career number two, but in the in-between.

"I know it sounds like it was a dramatic career shift," Ben tells me. "But I was performing while I was an executive director, so it happened gradually. There was no great aha moment. It was just a question of listening to myself. And I think we're all so busy with the minutiae of our lives that we sometimes fail to actually ask the big questions: 'What am I doing?' 'What makes me happy?' 'How do I want to spend my life?'"

Given his environment, Ben did not have the luxury of avoiding the big questions. "I had all of my friends dying," he explains. "It makes you think about what is important in your life. When you don't know if you're going to be alive, if the people you love are going to be alive."[4]

"Did you consult with anyone when you were thinking of making the switch?" I ask.

"I do remember one conversation I had [with my parents], and I was like, 'I'm thinking of quitting my job to go full-time with the Kinsey Sicks.' I think I was thirty-nine at the time. And my dad said, 'If you don't do it now, when are you going to do it?'"

"Did anyone try to talk you out of it?"

"There was not a single person who was meaningful in my life who did not embrace this on my behalf," he says with conviction.

I bring up another statement from Ben's Salon article: "I had worked damned hard to get where I was," Ben wrote. "My life was going to be meaningful no matter how miserable it made me."[5]

"Do you think your life was more meaningful when you were a lawyer?" I ask him.

"What I did before was extremely meaningful, and what I'm doing now is extremely meaningful too, in my opinion. But this one makes me happier," he says. "I wanted to be happy," he admits, like it's a confession. "I wanted to be as happy as I possibly could be. I could try to come up with something more complicated than that, but that's really it."

"I have to admit," I say to Ben, "it sounds like your career transition maybe wasn't that big of a deal, after all."

He immediately disagrees.

"No. No, it was a big, *big* deal to me. Because I had really had three careers [as a lawyer, an executive director, and a drag performer], each of which were dream jobs. So, the hard thing was not so much choosing the new dream but letting go of the old one."

He continues.

"You know, I have some nerve. I was doing really important work as a lawyer. And then I became executive director of the leading national LGBT organization. There were a small handful of jobs like that at the time. So, I really felt like, 'Who am I to turn away from this?' And it's not like I was doing something I hated or wasn't proud of. I was enormously proud of the work that I did. But then something came along that I loved more."

"It's kind of like a divorce on some level," he continues. "You've been with somebody. You go through life together, and then you find that you want to be single or you want to be with someone else. And it's hard to let go of something you've invested so much into, and that *is* valuable. You know, it's one thing if you divorce and you're like, 'Oh my God, that was horrible. How could I have ever been in that?' It's another thing when it's a relationship that had many good things. That's a difficult change to make."

Ben gives a chuckle, then a sigh. "It was a big deal to me to let go of something I loved in the hope that my new, greater love would succeed. It's not like there was a job opening to be a drag queen, like I could just apply for that job and get it. I'd have to create it. All three of the jobs I had were essentially jobs that hadn't existed before I created them. So, I just believed we could make the Kinsey Sicks work, but that doesn't mean that I *knew* we could. I just felt like I had to try."

In the great tradition of amateurism, Ben decided it would be good to try, even though he didn't know what would happen. He stepped off solid ground and learned to walk through sand and snow (metaphorically speaking) in high heels (literally). To make it even more difficult, when Ben decided to *go try*, he didn't give up a good or decent career; he gave up an important career. A career to be proud of. A career that was both meaningful and chock-full of the privileges afforded a "professional."

Don't forget, Ben was a graduate of Harvard Law School—the most prestigious professional school there is. He was a *double* Harvard graduate, actually, because he also graduated as an undergrad from Harvard College in 1981 (ironically, the same year doctors first identified HIV). So, despite being a marginalized gay man, Ben had what some would call pedigree. And like all established professionals, he had important things to lose—things like respect, wealth, and standing in society.

So, why did he give it all up? Why didn't he come to the same conclusion that Kabir Sehgal did, that he could remain a professional and become an amateur in addition? I think the answer is this: Ben gave up his profession because he found a love that no other love could match. He found a *great* love, and once he did, he could no longer offer time and energy to his lesser loves.

We know what Kabir has to teach us: that more is more, that multiple pursuits are mutually beneficial. What does Ben have to teach us? It's that less can also be more. It's that, sometimes, letting go of certain valuable things gains you more *more* valuable things—things like love, joy, and happiness.

In other words, you don't have to hold on to lesser interests just to keep them around—because someday they might benefit you. You're not required to cling to everything you've ever done just because you've invested time and money in those things. Even if you *like* those things, you have the right to let them go if you love something more.

An interesting addendum to Ben's story is that once he let himself go with his greater love, he figured out how to incorporate into it the things he valued from his old profession. He figured out how to sing, make people laugh, *and* get them to give a shit about gay people. He found that drag was, in many ways, a better venue for talking about the experiences of gay men—a better way to chip away at discrimination—than the law ever was.

"I could in some ways reach people more effectively as a singer and comic than as a policy person or talking head," he tells me. "There's something about the power of laughter and music . . . They're incredibly powerful tools to say provocative things." As Ben once put it another way, "Making people laugh is much more fun than suing them, and no less effective in making them think."[6]

"Do you think you would have arrived at the Kinsey Sicks without having been a lawyer first?" I ask him.

"I don't think the law really had anything to do with it," he replies. "I was never a lawyer's lawyer. I was an activist that got a Harvard law degree as a means to be taken seriously." He thinks for a moment. "But the hideously homophobic nonresponse to the AIDS crisis constantly threw it in my face that my life was without value . . . I was constantly contending with my perceived lack of humanity. I didn't have to be a lawyer to do that. I just had to be a sentient gay male," he says. "So, would I have arrived at the Kinsey Sicks if there hadn't been an AIDS crisis? I wish there was a control group so that I could have the answer to that one."

From this statement, I start to see Ben's decision to go full-time with the Kinsey Sicks as a self-affirming act. Perhaps also a life-affirming act. In the face of a world that said, through its silence, that his life had no value, Ben chose to do what he loved. This was a way of saying, *My life does have value.* It was a way of saying, *My loves are valid too.*

My experience in this world—my joy—matters too.

I matter too.

"And what's not to *love*?" Ben cheers in a singsong voice. "I get to use so many creative skills, and it just feels fantastic. I mean, the salary does *suck*. But once you have enough to eat and health care and all that, happiness is worth more. I often joke that I'm in the bottom five percent of my law-school class in terms of income and in the top five percent in terms of happiness. I'll take that exchange."

"What advice would you give someone who's fallen in love with a new dream and now has to contend with that?" I ask.

"I guess I'd say, don't dismiss what you're feeling. Take it seriously. Seriously ask yourself, 'If not now, when?' And if the thought keeps waking you up—keeps *tickling* you—listen. Listen to what your heart's telling you." Unable to repress Rachel any longer, Ben breaks out into song. "And I'd tell them, don't become a singing drag queen. Because. That. Job's. *Takennn!*"

AMATOR: "LOVER OF"

As we edge toward the end of this book, it's time to return to the beginning—to the original, positive meaning of the designation "amateur."

Amator: the one who loves.

A great master amateur keeps always at the forefront of her mind the spirit of the original amateur—the one who does what she does because she loves it. She factors joy and happiness into her life. She allows herself to make at least some crucial career decisions based not on what's logical or strategic, but on what *feels right*. She will certainly do some activities out of necessity, as we all do, but she'll also do some activities just because she wants to do them. No further justification necessary.

Now, encouraging people to do what they love is no new thing. Our culture constantly tells people to do what they love. Ideally, for a living. *Find a job you love, and you'll never work a day in your life.* It's one of our American ideals. But anyone who's grown to adulthood in this culture knows that it's a superficial ideal, at best. It's an ideal we appear to believe in, but just below the surface we're deeply conflicted about it.

That's because we, as a culture, also believe a contradictory thing: that only a handful of careers are really good. Only a few paths lead to a life that's good in all respects. So, many of us find ourselves in a protracted, often painful quandary: *Do what you love . . . as long as it's one of these five things.* It's a mixed message that confuses the senses. We hear a call to freedom but see only hedged paths. We're told to go wherever we want to go in a world of one-way streets. That makes for a long and confusing journey.

Ben Schatz referenced this cultural quandary in an interview he gave the *Harvard Crimson* in 2018. In it, he said, "It's very tempting when you're at Harvard to assume that there are really only four careers: business, law, medicine, or academia."[7] Through this statement he implied that this—the professional paradigm—is at least partially why it took him forty years to do what he loved.

If you're lucky and you grow up with adults who are open-minded, you might be aware of more than four or five viable career paths. You might know of ten. But the majority of those paths will still be the professions. And the rest? You'll be encouraged to do those only if you really, really, *really* want to.

⁕ ⁕ ⁕

To be clear, I'm not saying that the professions are unlovable. Certain people would gleefully practice medicine, for example, even if it weren't a respectable profession. But the majority of the *actual work* (not imagined work) associated with the professions is hard to love. Does anyone really love composing emails, making follow-up calls, getting permits, sterilizing equipment, reviewing intake forms, making financial models, and so on?

Or a better question is: Are these anyone's *great* loves?

These tasks are tolerable to most and enjoyable to some. But love—*great* love—is a different thing. It's different in its substance. It's not wind or water eroding a person from the outside. It's a fiery spark from within. It's a spontaneous reaction that arises when the right elements meet in the soul. Imagination, adventure, beauty, mystery—these are the ingredients that make great loves.

The craft of amateurism shows us how to get at *this* kind of love—and make it into work. Amateurism does this by asking you to do everything backward. Instead of starting with the list of career options society gives you and then steadily working toward the one you think you *might* love eventually, amateurism asks you to start with your current, innate, *natural* loves. First step: mine your soul for what you already love, now.

Then take those loves seriously. Take them seriously no matter how far they deviate from society's preordained career paths. At the beginning of this book, I said that the primary core competency of a master amateur is learning to take one's own impulses seriously. Love is the most important impulse we have, so a great master amateur will take *it* seriously, most of all.

Once you consider them seriously, you'll find that some of your loves beg to *become something*. They want to manifest—to become something tangible. This is your opportunity to make your love your work. Turn your love into a project, a pursuit, a practice, or even a persona like "Rachel." Your work can be anything, now, as long as it takes your love—a most immaterial thing—and materializes it.

A HEART FULL OF CLOUDS

During the summer of 1783, the sky over England was a frightful sight to see. From May to August of that year, a thick, murky haze cloaked the whole of the British Isles, turning its once-blue sky the color of burnt milk. At night, the stars showed a flashy, unnatural twinkle. Today, we know the haze was caused by volcanic ash floating over England from Iceland. But at the time, the British people knew it only as the "Great Fogg."[8]

That summer, an eleven-year-old boy named Luke Howard was living at boarding school in the small medieval town of Burford, England. He had never seen a sight like the skies of 1783. His fascination with the Great Fogg reached its zenith on August 18, when, just after sunset, a fiery meteor streaked across the milky sky. While his schoolmates shrieked and pointed to the heavens, Luke Howard, the future father of meteorology, ran to his journal and described the streak with harrowing precision.

From that day on, Luke Howard had a love affair with the sky. "His lifelong passion," his biographer, Richard Hamblyn, later wrote, "was for staring out of the window at the sky."[9]

For over three decades of his life, Luke Howard recorded the skies over England nearly every single day. He produced the most thorough accounting of English weather ever seen at the time. His records included thermometer and barometer readings (data rarely captured in that day) as well as detailed descriptions of his observations. His descriptions of clouds—his favorite aerial objects—read more like love letters than weather observations. "The sky about sunset was overspread with . . . clouds," he once recorded, "beautifully tinged with flame colour—red and violet."[10] When the beauty of the clouds could not be captured in words, he'd paint their forms in watercolor.

Through his collection of data, observations, and paintings, Luke Howard came to invent the modern discipline of meteorology. He proved that the sky, particularly clouds, could be understood from a *scientific* perspective. Before Luke, natural scientists believed clouds to be "airy nothings."[11] And while clouds were known to produce rain, the cloud-to-rain process seemed so transient, scientists thought it would never stand up to rigorous study.

Luke proved that clouds could be studied, they could be organized just like plants and animals were, and they could teach us invisible truths about the atmosphere. To prove these things, he first created a nomenclature for cloud types. He gave the clouds names. He named the four fundamental cloud types that he'd observed—from which all other clouds derive—*cirrus*, *cumulus*, *stratus*, and *nimbus*.

Cirrus (Latin for "fiber") is the wispy cloud. *Cumulus* (Latin for "pile") is the fluffy white cloud. *Stratus* (Latin for "layer") is the overcast cloud. And *nimbus* (Latin for "rain") is the rain cloud.

From these four fundamental forms, scientists could consistently identify any variety of cloud they saw in the moment. The high-altitude, paper-thin cloud that creates a halo around the moon at night came to be called *cirrostratus* because it's a transitional form between *cirrus* and *stratus*. The dense, towering cloud responsible for thunder came to be known as *cumulonimbus* because it's a combination of *cumulus* and *nimbus*.

Unlike the purely fanciful names clouds had born for thousands of years (names like "woolly," "buttermilk," "mare's tails," "mackerel skies," and "towers and castles"), Luke's names were decidedly scientific.[12] They followed the Linnaean principles of classification. They could be mixed and matched to describe hybrids and intermediary forms. They were Latin so as to be universal and timeless—a success, I'd say, as they're still the names we call the clouds today.

༄ ༄ ༄

Luke first presented his nomenclature for clouds in 1802 to the Askesian Society in London. The Askesian Society was one of the great debating societies for scientists of the time, and its lectures were popular entertainment for the public. Any man of leisure with a beaker and a theory could walk on stage and show his experiments to an enthusiastic audience of scientists, laypeople, and children alike. But even by these inclusive standards, Luke's audience in 1802 did not take him seriously. They looked upon him, his biographer wrote, as "an unknown, amateur cloud-watcher."[13]

Luke Howard was indeed an amateur cloud-watcher. He had no education in the natural sciences and never pursued a job in the field. To name the clouds, he relied on the little Latin he'd learned as a schoolboy. He received no formal mentorship or guidance in the natural sciences; everything he knew about the sky came from his own observations. As far as we know, he only observed the sky because he couldn't take his eyes off it.

By trade, Luke was a "retail chemist," meaning he manufactured industrial chemicals and sold them to businesses. He'd suffered a grueling, seven-year apprenticeship to learn this trade and reportedly hated the job ever after. But in the long run, Luke's day job helped him devote more and more time to his great loves: cirrus, cumulus, stratus, and nimbus. In midlife, he'd earned enough money to purchase a comfortable home in Plaistow, East London, and to build an observatory on the top floor. He installed "high windows [that] looked out upon the sky in every direction of the compass." And there, "amid his books, his young children and his increasing sense of fulfilment, Luke Howard grew happier and happier."[14]

When he died, aged ninety-one, Luke had transcended the initial sideways glances he received at the Askesian Society. The scientific community adopted his nomenclature for clouds within his lifetime, and his collected lectures were published in 1837 as the first meteorological textbook. His magnum opus, *The Climate of London*, was the first-ever in-depth analysis of urban weather. In it, he identified the phenomenon of "city fog" (what we now call smog), and "urban heat"—an increase in atmospheric temperature due to the burning of fossil fuels.

At his funeral, Luke's eldest son, Robert, eulogized his father, not by recounting his accomplishments, but by recounting his loves. "Those who lived with him will not soon forget his interest in the appearance of the sky," Robert said. "Whether at morning, noon, or night, he would go out to look around on the heavens, and notice the changes going on . . . A beautiful sunset was a real and intense delight to him; he would stand at the window, change his position, go out of doors and watch it to the last lingering ray."[15]

A VAGABOND IN THE AIR

On a bright December morning in 1920, Amelia Earhart and her father, Edwin Earhart, attended an air show in Long Beach, California. The show featured Frank Hawks, a renowned World War I pilot and "fast flying" enthusiast. The planes flying high and fast gripped Amelia, instantly. Her father, noticing his daughter's intense interest in the scene, offered Frank Hawks ten dollars to take her up and fly her around for ten minutes.

"As soon as we left the ground," Amelia later wrote in her autobiography, *The Fun of It*, "I knew myself had to fly." She went home that evening and softballed her new obsession to her family. "'I think I'd like to learn to fly,' I told the family casually that evening, knowing full well I'd die if I didn't."[16]

Eight years after that first flight, Amelia Earhart gained worldwide fame as the first woman to fly across the Atlantic Ocean. She'd always deprecate this first trip across the Atlantic—in which she was a passenger, not the pilot—as "a pleasant interlude" and "primarily a vacation."[17] Her life motto became "There is more to life than being a passenger." True to her motto, four years after her first transatlantic flight, she became the first woman (and the second person ever) to fly the Atlantic solo.[18]

In 1937, Amelia's life was cut short on a failed attempt to circumnavigate the globe. But before that, she also became the first woman to fly solo nonstop across the continental United States and the first person to fly solo from Hawaii to the US mainland. She took so much visceral pleasure in the Hawaii flight that halfway through she broke out a thermos of hot chocolate and tuned her radio to a broadcast of the Metropolitan Opera.

When Amelia attended that air show in 1920, no one would have pegged her for an aviation pioneer in the making. No one expected much of her. At the time, she was a twenty-three-year-old Columbia University dropout who eked out a living as a nurse's aide. She was a *double* Columbia University dropout, actually; she abandoned a premed degree in 1920 and a physics degree in 1924, describing the second attempt as futile from the start. "There was a quiz in physics every week," she later wrote. "When I could not answer questions properly I inserted a little French poetry."[19]

Amelia always lacked focus in our contemporary sense. She never set concrete goals for herself and seemed to give up on things easily. She was impulsive in that way we call brave or stupid depending on the situation. But, it seems, when she found flying, she found an impulse she could take seriously. She found an activity in which she could be impetuous in a laser-focused way—a combination that intoxicated her from the start.

So, to fund her new (and very expensive) hobby, Amelia abandoned nursing for a slurry of more-lucrative jobs. She worked as a social worker and as a stenographer for a local telephone company. She did a bit of commercial photography, truck driving, and mining in Nevada. Though she'd never have access to professional flight schools (those were for military personnel only), she estimated that if she saved $1,000, she could pay a pilot returning from war to teach her privately.

Amelia did indeed earn enough money—$1,000 plus extra—to recruit esteemed female pilot Neta Snook as her private instructor (Neta was the first woman ever to start an aviation business). Neta taught Amelia to fly and helped her find a secondhand biplane for sale. Amelia purchased the bright-yellow biplane on her twenty-fifth birthday and named it the *Canary*. Three months later, she flew the *Canary* to an altitude of fourteen thousand feet, setting her first of many world records for female pilots.

※ ※ ※

For the first decade or so of Amelia Earhart's aviation career, she seemed to be flying purely on instinct. She loved the sensation of flying and picked her flights based on their sensory appeal. She did not pick them strategically; she was not building toward the goal of becoming the best female pilot in the world. Even in the afterglow of her historic 1928 transatlantic flight (the one in which she was a passenger), she admitted, "I still had no plan for myself. Should I return to social work, or find something to do in aviation? I didn't know—nor care. For the moment all I wished to do in the world was to be a vagabond in the air."[20]

But when Amelia started to seriously consider attempting the second-ever solo flight across the Atlantic, she seemed pressed more and more to explain why. Why attempt something so ambitious... if you're *not* ambitious? People found her aimless excellence hard to understand. Even her husband, who typically supported Amelia's hobby, wrote to her before a particularly dangerous flight and asked her why she wanted to do it. Unable, or unwilling, to justify her desires, Amelia simply wrote back, "I want to do it because I want to do it."[21]

In her autobiography, *The Fun of It*, Amelia does the most thoughtful self-reflection she ever would on the question of why. But even here, she gives little reason other than "I did it because I wanted to do it." "Ever since my first crossing [of the Atlantic] . . . ," she wrote, "when I was merely a passenger, I have wanted to attempt a solo flight. Then, a few months ago I decided upon it seriously . . . It was clear in my mind that I was undertaking the flight because I loved flying. I chose to fly the Atlantic because I wanted to."[22]

For Amelia Earhart, *loving to do something* was a complete and sufficient reason to do it. The act did not need to lead to anything else. A joyful act is not a means to an end—it's an end in and of itself. Don't try to justify it, Amelia seems to have said. Joy upends justification. Just go be a vagabond in the air. For the joy, for the love, for the *fun* of it!

TEN THOUSAND WAYS TO LOVE THE SKY

One of the most important skills a master amateur knows is how to invoke the spirit of the original amateur—the one who does what he loves just because he loves it. Master amateurs are experts at letting their loves guide them to what *could* be. Instead of surveying the work landscape that already exists and trying to fit themselves into it, they let their loves show them what work *could* exist instead.

Remember, there was a time not so long ago when careers as commonplace as airplane pilot and meteorologist were unheard of. These would have made no one's top-ten list (or even top-hundred list) of viable work options. Until, of course, amateurs made them viable.

In Luke Howard's time, there was no preexisting career path in meteorology for anyone to find or follow. It simply didn't exist. So, the directive to "find a career you love" wouldn't have worked for Luke. In fact, it would have been a great hinderance to him. That line of thinking presupposes that all viable careers already exist, which they do not.

Instead, Luke Howard did what he enjoyed, and the career found him.

Now, a quick aside. When I picked Luke Howard and Amelia Earhart as the historical examples for this chapter, I chose them because they were both obviously motivated by love. Only later did I realize that Luke and Amelia essentially loved the same thing: the sky. Their contributions to society were so different, I initially didn't notice this connection at all.

That's because although they were utterly fascinated by the same thing, they manifested their fascination in completely different ways based on their personalities. Luke was pensive and meticulous. He loved the sky, but he also loved contemplation and observation. So, he manifested his love for the sky by watching it more closely than anyone ever had before.

Amelia, on the other hand, was spontaneous and fearless. She would never have had the patience to name the clouds. She loved adventure as much as she loved the sky. So, for her, the natural manifestation of her love was continent-hopping.

Sophie Blanchard, a nineteenth-century amateur balloonist who suffered from debilitating anxiety, was said to be "only comfortable in the air."[23] She loved the sky, and she also loved the serene silence she found up in the air. Her two loves, combined, made her a pioneer of peaceful hot-air ballooning.[24]

David Hoadley, a self-taught expert on tornadoes, became intensely interested in the power of bad weather when, as a kid, a windstorm knocked out the power in his hometown. He loved the sky and also obsessed over the destructive power of Mother Nature. These two obsessions, combined, made him the first-ever storm chaser.[25]

This is all to say that if you've ever thought there are only so many things in this world to love, that all the great loves must be taken, think again. Countless people could love the same thing and each manifest their love in a unique, important way. There are probably ten thousand ways to love the sky, alone. One of those ways could be yours.

CHAPTER 10

CURIOSITY

I have no special talents. I am only passionately curious.
—Albert Einstein

THE RANDOM WALK

I found Jonathon Keats online (as people find each other nowadays) when his phantasmagoric Wikipedia page caught my eye. I reached out to him on social media (as people do nowadays) only to learn that he lives in my neighborhood and that, back in the '80s, my mother was his high school English teacher.

The absurdity of this, my last interview for this book, continued when Jonathon picked NOOK café in the Russian Hill district of San Francisco as the site of our interview. NOOK is a stunted café, a space jammed up onto a street corner by Powell-Hyde cable cars making too-close right turns. It's like a potted plant making do with a too-small pot.

When Jonathon arrives at NOOK to meet me, he looks exactly how I'd hoped he would. He's wearing a purple checkered bow tie and a tweed jacket. He has with him a beat brown leather bag with a flap-over—the kind of bag that flagrantly intellectual men carry. His spectacles glint in the afternoon light and his voice is soft, almost too soft given the *clang-a-rang* of cable cars invading our personal space.

Jonathon Keats is an experimental philosopher. Emphasis on *experimental*. He does not know what that job title means. He only knows that he chose it in reference to the holistic thinkers of the past—the men who were sometimes called "experimental philosophers," other times "natural philosophers," and very oftentimes "amateurs."

He, more than any other master amateur I've profiled in this book, will tell you with certainty that he does not know what he's doing and that's exactly why he's doing it. He does not know what he's doing on both a large and a small scale. He does not have a grand plan for his life or work, and he more often than not lacks basic, practical understanding of what he's tinkering with right in front of him.

But this cluelessness is not an accident. This is ignorance by design.

In terms of what he actually *does*, Jonathon Keats manufactures uncertainty—for himself and for others—through the creation of thought experiments. The best way to get a sense of what *thought experiments* means is to see them listed in rapid succession, without context or comment.

So.

Here we go.

In 2002, Jonathon attempted to pass the mathematical law of identity ($A = A$) as statutory law in Berkeley, California. The law proposed that "every entity shall be identical to itself" and any entity caught *not* being itself would incur a fine of one-tenth of one cent. The law was "too weird for Berkeley" and didn't pass.[1]

In 2003, he devised a plan to survive his own death by copyrighting his brain. Through established copyright law, he'd retain intellectual-property rights on his thoughts for seventy years after his death, attaining temporary immortality and fulfilling Descartes's philosophical proclamation "I think, therefore I am."

He's composed a "honeybee ballet" by planting a garden in such a way that bees had the appearance of dancing with each other as they pollinated the flowers.

He's written "the longest story ever told." It's a nine-word story printed in increasingly UV-resistant ink that, as it's exposed to sunlight, reveals one word per century.

He's officiated "quantum marriages," whereby people in love skip the legal paperwork and get their subatomic particles entangled across all space and time. According to physics, quantum entanglement disappears when it is observed, however, so the existence of these marriages is based on faith alone.

He's drawn up housing blueprints for theoretical real estate in the fourth dimension. One hundred and seventy-two 4-D houses were purchased at his first-ever interdimensional open house.

And perhaps most famously, Jonathon ran a series of laboratory experiments in 2004 to determine where on the evolutionary tree of life he could place God. Is God an animal? A plant? A fungus? Due to its ecstatic growth when exposed to religious chanting, Jonathon determined that God is a type of cyanobacteria. When a reporter questioned him on his understanding of the disciplines involved in the experiments, Jonathon responded, "A sort of profound ignorance is a good working methodology, at least for me."[2]

Most journalists and critics call Jonathon Keats an absurdist—someone who tries to startle people out of their ordinary life by confronting them with something ridiculous. The *New Yorker*, perhaps more kindly, calls him a "poet of ideas."[3] He would forgive you for calling him a nutcase. He *is* a nutcase in the sense that he's a devout anti-assumptionist. He tries to live without relying on even basic assumptions about anything. And if you'd like, he'll create for you a situation that you can't process by relying on your assumptions, so you'll have to adapt and process it some other way.

The skill of being able to adapt without the use of assumptions is critically important to humanity's survival in the future. Our long-held assumptions about society, reality, and so on are only going to break down faster and faster from here (just wait until we find aliens).

Paradoxically, this is a skill that we've, for the most part, lost in our constant reupping of status quos.

But there's hope. According to Jonathon Keats, this critically important skill can make a comeback. Because it's not really lost. It's just living in exile in the realm of the ignorant and the incompetent. It's living over in the land of amateurs.

༄ ༄ ༄

As I sip my lemonade and do the equivalent of squint with my ears, Jonathon explains to me in a gentle voice that it all started with rocks.

"One day, when I was around six years old, I decided to sell rocks. A lot of children paint rocks or in some way try to make them special. I didn't make anything at all of the rocks other than take them off the ground, put them onto a table, and set it up in the driveway of our house where more or less nobody walked by."

"Why did you do that?" I ask him.

"My father was a stockbroker, and it was one of the most baffling things for a six-year-old to try to understand what that entailed, and more generally, to try to make sense of what people do all day working for money. Our whole economic system is so incredibly obvious to grown-ups that I think they have little time, patience, or inclination to explain it. Therefore, I don't think they really understand it very well themselves." Jonathon takes a sip of his tea. "So, that was my way of trying to figure it out. And it's really what I've been doing ever since—figuring out active ways to explore the systems operating in our society that are so fundamental as to be taken for granted."

"What other systems do you think we take for granted?"

"The academic system is certainly one," he says. "When I went to [Amherst College to study philosophy], I had taken for granted that the study of philosophy would be about learning to think and ask big questions and be in conversation . . . and it wasn't anything like that. It was dry and abstruse and fundamentally inaccessible to anyone who didn't have training."

Jonathon took issue, in particular, with what philosophy the discipline had done to the thought experiment—the thing that originally interested him in philosophy. "In studying philosophy, I was particularly interested in the thought experiment as a mode of exploration, but I found out I wasn't interested in it in the way that it actually is used within the discipline."

How is it used within the discipline? It's a mode by which to argue a point, Jonathon explains to me. It's a tool that philosophers use to force others into a position where they have to admit that the philosopher's conclusion about the world is right.

"You didn't like that approach?" I ask him.

"It's not that I didn't like it. It's that I don't have a point that I am setting out to make. I'm interested in the question, not the answer. And if you come to some sort of conclusion or some sort of answer, to me it's only as interesting as the questions that again arise."

In other words, Jonathon couldn't align himself with philosophy the discipline, because the enterprise was too intent on eliminating questions. He wanted to stay with the questions. He wanted to stay in the state of not knowing—not as some sort of self-flagellation but because, for him, there's joy in the state of not knowing. As long as you don't know, you always *want to know*. To me, Jonathon's like a child with no Christmas presents but a permanent abundance of Christmas Eve anticipation.

"An awareness of what I don't know actually is incredibly exhilarating to me. Not knowing is something that I really seek," he says as some baseball-capped tourists disembark a cable car outside. "That's why I try to prototype free spaces where we can all let our guard down and just be in a space where certainty is undetermined."

A space where certainty is undetermined.

What does that mean?

Let me give you an example.

In 2007, Jonathon opened his first movie theater for plants. I say "first" because he ultimately opened three movie theaters: one that showed porn, one that showed travel documentaries, and one that showed sci-fi movies. *For plants.* In the porn theater, projectors beamed down videos of pollination acts onto the leaves of ninety rhododendrons. In the travel-doc theater, an audience of American ficus and palm trees watched a beautiful Italian sky pass from morning into night. In the sci-fi theater, house plants went on an interstellar journey as the room filled with the light of a yellow dwarf, then a red giant, then a neutron star.

Of course, people were also invited to watch the plants . . . watch the movies. In these theaters, the human onlookers experienced (most likely for the first time) an entertainment experience *not* designed for them. They watched a movie made without them in mind. People are not the center of these worlds that Jonathon created, however small they may be. So, for a brief moment, these people watching plants don't know what to think.

Is this what movie watching is like? they wonder.

Do I look like that fern when I watch a movie?
Am I that . . . sedentary?
Do I . . . matter . . . here?
A space where certainty is undetermined.

I have a question that's been brewing in my mind for a long time now. I've been waiting for just the right master amateur to pose it to, and after Jonathon tells me about his indeterminate movie theaters for plants, I decide he's the one.

"Jonathon," I ask, "do you think people cling to academic degrees and certifications and job titles because, deep down, they're scared?" I realize I should have practiced this question before asking it. I try to clarify. "I mean, we're such a goal-oriented society now. We're taught to always have a concrete goal in mind—like a degree or a promotion or whatever. And it's like, if you're working hard but you don't know exactly what you're working towards, then you're making some kind of terrible mistake. But," I offer, "don't you think that's just fear?"

Jonathon chuckles softly.

"Yes. I believe that we have become increasingly a goal-oriented society in terms of both how we behave and what we value. What we value is the *proof of work*." He sips the last bit of his tea. "And yet, at the same time, I think we are adrift. Because the goals we set for ourselves tend to be superficial and, in my opinion, arbitrary. That arbitrariness is born out of an existential crisis that we are having individually and societally, where we will try anything we can to avoid what we fear most, dread most."

Jonathon doesn't have to say what that thing is we fear most, dread most. I know what that thing is. It's the unknown.

"What do you think would help?"

"Well, I think what is needed are more curious amateurs in the true and old sense of the word—people who are not necessarily working toward a goal but working simply out of their own interest, pursuing their own curiosity," he replies. "We need more mechanisms by which amateurism is encouraged. The pedagogy of amateurism is inherently a paradoxical thing, but it's an essential thing for us to have and to encourage more of."

Perhaps amateurs—those who embrace not knowing—are best equipped to lead us into an unknowable future without fear.

"For my work," he states, "being an amateur is absolutely essential. The mix of media, the mix of disciplines, the mix of ideas necessary to start out a thought process in one place and allow it to move freely to all the other places it wants to go—there's no training in the world that would prepare me for that. Any training might actually limit the gamut of where it can go. Training is going to give you assumptions and make it very hard for you to see them. So, I made a point of not committing to any given area of expertise or to any given methodology . . . I'm just committed to being an amateur."

"I'm curious," I ask, "when you're committed to being an amateur, what does your process—the making of your work—actually look like?"

"Well, I would say a great deal of my process is subsidized by Google and eBay." He giggles. "But I think the more interesting answer might be that *serendipity* is as important to my process as traditional learning and research is. And by *serendipity* I mean I really value the subject matters, the information, the data that I stumble upon while looking for something else."

"I am always working on many projects at once," he continues. "So, I am in many different areas of knowledge and expertise simultaneously. I also go about my research very circuitously. I look at the books *next to* the book on the shelf. So,

I find myself always going places I never would have thought of when I started."

The cable cars turn less and less frequently as this afternoon inches toward evening.

"What advice would you give someone who wants to commit to amateurism?" I ask.

"Go on the random walk through as many different realms as possible as a matter of general curiosity. I've always been driven by curiosity more than anything else—essentially what any child is driven by. I'm still a child selling rocks in many ways. I just didn't ever get around to growing up."

With this, my interview with Jonathon Keats is over. We gather up our things and maneuver to the door. We step out onto the smooshed-up street corner of Jackson and Hyde. We say our goodbyes, and Jonathon turns to go. "I want you to know," he boasts loudly for the first time, "I'm always getting better at being worse at research!"

I'm the one who giggles this time. I just might like to get better at being worse too.

THE CHILDREN IN THE ROOM

A great master amateur lets his curiosity take him on a journey—a *real* journey, the kind that has no destination in mind. He trusts that curiosity is a wiser guide than are his learned assumptions about "how things are." His mind is present in the moment with his sincerest interests. It's not somewhere out there with society's preconceived notions about rightness and wrongness, about smart moves and foolish moves.

A great master amateur is unafraid to set out on a journey without knowing where it will lead, because wherever genuine interest takes him is a valuable place to go. To him, there are not worthy destinations and unworthy destinations. The place we call "success" is a good place to go. The place we call "failure" is also a good place to go. Back to the beginning is a good place too. *Hopefully,* he wishes, *I will visit every place at least once.* It is a journey, after all.

Now, if curiosity is going to be our guide on this journey, let's talk about what it really means. The dictionary definition of *curiosity* is "a strong desire to know or learn something." This definition captures the reason why curiosity is special enough to be our guide: it's a strong desire to know—that precludes ever actually knowing. It's a motivating force that lasts forever as long as it's never fulfilled.

As I said earlier in this chapter, as long as you don't know, you always *want to know.* Put another way, if you don't abandon curiosity, curiosity won't abandon you.

Once you believe you know something, you're no longer curious about it. You'll move, intentionally or not, into a defensive position once you believe you know. You'll turn from wanting to learn more about the thing that interests you to warding off any new information that might threaten your *achievement* of knowing. Certainty becomes something to defend, something to keep from losing. This is a fearful stance, whether experts in their field know it or not. The good news is, curious amateurs are happy to show experts how difficult it is to fear anything when you *wonder* about everything.

※ ※ ※

"A strong desire to know or learn something." That's the first definition of the word *curiosity.*

There's also a second definition.

Curiosity: "a strange or unusual object or fact."

An oddity, an outlier, a quirk, a weird phenomenon, a strange encounter—anything specific and interesting is also a "curiosity." The Great Fogg of 1783 was a curiosity. Julia

Domna's hairstyle was a curiosity. Forrest's grandfather's ability to get around town without being able to see was a curiosity. Some of our greatest amateurs embarked on their own journeys of exploration after an encounter with something inexplicable. So, these curiosities—the strange or unusual objects or facts of life—are our guides too.

The thing is, from the perspective of the wide-eyed amateur, a thing doesn't have to be truly unusual to inspire awe. It doesn't have to be rare or unfamiliar. Anything can be seen as an object of fascination. You don't have to wait for a close encounter to start exploring your world.

All things, when unpacked and understood for what they really are, are curiosities. Pull back the veil of familiarity, and everything around us is amazing and worthy of exploration. As the great scientist Albert Einstein said it, "There are only two ways to live your life. One is as though nothing is a miracle. The other is as though everything is a miracle."[4]

꼽 꼽 꼽

Another great scientist from the past exemplifies how to live in awareness of the miraculous nature of everything. That scientist's name was Michael Faraday, and he was an amateur. He was self-taught in physics and chemistry—the disciplines he would revolutionize—and his knowledge of math never exceeded simple algebra. Despite this, he discovered (through experimentation) the physical laws that explain how electromagnetism works. He discovered the principles of electromagnetic rotation and electromagnetic induction, the first of which led to the invention of the electric motor while the second laid the groundwork for the practical applications of electricity that define our society today.

He also made another kind of contribution to society. He explained to the people of his time, most notably children, in simple, nonacademic language they could understand, how complex physical processes work. During the Christmas season of 1860 to 1861, Michael Faraday gave a series of popular lectures for children at the Royal Institution in London. The topic of these lectures? An everyday, ordinary candle. The kind of candle those children burned each night beside their beds—a thing that was, in Jonathon Keats's term, *taken for granted*, if anything ever was.

But by looking at a candle, Faraday explained, one can see all the processes that govern the universe. The chemical combustion that causes *fire* is just like the combustion that creates *life*. The candlewick is excellent in its way, as it contains all the elements needed for the fire to live. The wick does not vanish when it is burned either. It transforms into airborne carbon—carbon that feeds the plants that feed *you*.

The kids who attended those Christmas lectures likely left thinking they'd never seen anything as amazing as a candle, as seen through Michael Faraday's eyes. It's all there, he showed, once you peel back the layers of ordinariness: the awe-inspiring interconnectedness of everything. He chose a candle to explore, but it could have been anything. As Nobel Prize–winning physicist Richard Feynman once wrote, the point of Faraday's Christmas lectures was to show that "no matter what you look at, if you look at it closely enough, you are involved in the entire universe."[5]

Today, many people believe that Michael Faraday's ability to see the world with such fascination—some might even say innocence—was due in part to his amateurism. He was not conditioned to think that some things are worthy of study and other things are not. He was not trained to speak in jargon and see expertise as an accomplishment. He still inhabited his original, untaught state—the place we all are in before we learn.

We master amateurs can hope to be great like Michael Faraday. But it's enough, I think, to hope to be like the children in his audience. It's enough to aspire to retain receptivity to wonder. Because we are not hardened experts. We are curious beginners, primed to be amazed. Professionals may be the adults in the room, but master amateurs are the children in the room, and we need both—adults and children—to keep the wheel of progress turning.

We need some people who care about the journey to balance out our society's borderline obsessive focus on goals, proofs of work, and destinations. We need some people who can still access innocence to buoy a world drowning in disenchantment. We need some people for whom the achievement of knowing could never hold a candle to a candle.

A CONSUMMATE AMATEUR

On a brisk summer day in 1811, fifteen-year-old Joseph Anning flung open the weather-beaten door of his family home and called out for his little sister. Twelve-year-old Mary Anning emerged from their father's old workshop and sat down to listen. Joseph told her he'd just been out to the coastal cliffs that border Lyme Regis, their hometown. A blustery storm—one typical of the southern coast of England—had just come and gone.

In the new rock exposed by the storm, Joseph said, he saw something strange. It *glistened*. Mary's eyes widened. It was a skull, he insisted. A *humungous* skull. It measured four feet long, he estimated, with room for some two hundred teeth.

Mary marveled. She'd seen some incredible things inch out of the shale and limestone that lined their coastal bluffs. But nothing *that big*. The two children surmised it was the head of a crocodile or a massive lizard. A petrified lizard skull (while undeniably cool) was not entirely unheard of in Lyme Regis. The hardscrabble beach town sat along one of the most erosion-prone coastlines in the world. And whenever a storm passed through, the cliffs would crumble to reveal a treasure trove of animals turned to stone.

Unfortunately, Joseph explained to Mary, he had no time to chip the skull out of the rock himself. He needed to get back to his upholstery apprenticeship; the children's father had just died, and they desperately needed money. So, Joseph suggested that Mary excavate it herself.

Mary heartily agreed. She was thrilled to excavate this creature, and at twelve years old, she was highly qualified to do so. From the time she could walk, her father, Richard, had taken her out to the beach to rummage for oddities. She'd carefully pick at the loose bits of cliff to see what strange things hid inside. Together, Mary and her father found fish skeletons, petrified squid, and the spiral casings of ancient mollusks. Today, we know these oddities were fossils—the preserved remains of creatures that lived long ago. But at that time, they were known as curios—objects of modest value and enormous fascination.

Mary spent the whole of her young life collecting curios. She'd sell the beautiful ones to tourists passing through Lyme Regis. Richard showed her how to polish shells so they sparkled and how to crack open ammonites to expose their inner crystalline structures. By the time she turned six, Richard had fashioned Mary a set of tiny tools so she could do all the work herself.

So, without hesitation, Mary ran to the spot on the cliffs where her brother indicated the skull would be. Her pick, chisel, and hammer bounced around in a rucksack tied to her skirt. She located the skull, and after another rageful storm came and went, she picked out the faint outline of a skeleton. Over the course of a year, Mary gingerly chipped away at the brittle limestone to reveal the creature's complete, connected skeleton. In total, it measured seventeen feet long.

Once the object was exposed, Mary knew it was no crocodile or lizard. The creature's head was reptilian, but it also had a pointed snout like a swordfish. Its eye sockets were huge, suggesting the creature had freaky bug eyes. Its body was most like an eel, but it also had two sets of flippers like a dolphin.

Mary could not say what it was, but she knew this creature should be preserved. So, she asked some men from town to help her move the fossil slabs back to her father's workshop. The men saw the creature and recoiled. They couldn't believe what they saw, and word of the find spread all over Lyme Regis. *Have you heard?* the townspeople must have whispered. *Richard Anning's little girl has found a monster.*

༃ ༃ ༃

Soon enough, word spread all the way to London that something special had been found in Lyme Regis. Mary sold the slabs to a collector, who then sold them to the British Museum, and at the museum, Mary's monster was renamed *Ichthyosaurus*. *Ichthyosaurus* was determined to have lived about two hundred million years ago. It was not quite a fish and not quite a reptile. It was, instead, a heresy fixed in stone.

Ichthyosaurus called into question many gospel truths of the time. Namely, that the Earth was a few thousand years old, and that every type of creature that ever existed, existed now. These were foundational beliefs in the early nineteenth century; even the most learned people believed—firmly—that species did not change, spring up spontaneously, or disappear into nothingness. If a species seemed to appear or disappear, it had simply moved into or out of an unexplored part of the world.

The first scientist to seriously propose that some species went extinct was famed French naturalist Georges Cuvier.

At almost the exact same time Mary dug up *Ichthyosaurus*, Georges Cuvier published his writings theorizing that, occasionally, catastrophic flooding events wiped out entire species. He pointed to the fossilized remains of mammoths as evidence. In academic circles, his theory gained traction, and "catastrophism" became the leading theory of extinction for the first half of the nineteenth century. Riding the success of his theory, Georges Cuvier became the undisputed authority figure in the new field of paleontology.

If any man has ever been a consummate professional, that man was Georges Cuvier. He was born into a family that could afford the best education. Georges attended gymnasium (Europe's form of elementary and secondary school) as a child and received private tutelage in Latin, Greek, mathematics, history, and geography. As a teenager, he attended the prestigious Caroline Academy in Stuttgart, Germany, where he studied the natural sciences and became fluent in many modern European languages.

Upon graduation, Georges moved to Paris and became a fellow of the Institut de France, an elite French learning society, as well as a professor of natural history at the Collège de France. He held an unbroken series of professorships in his lifetime and reigned supreme in Europe's members-only learning societies.

Mary Anning was, on the other hand, a consummate amateur. She received no formal education whatsoever and taught herself to read and write using the Bible available to her at Sunday school. She learned to excavate fossils without damaging them by trying different techniques to see what worked. She was fortunate that her father taught her basic handy skills—skills she'd adapt and evolve to meet whatever need confronted her in the field.

To understand the anatomy of the fossilized creatures she dug up, Mary dissected fish she caught from the sea. She didn't own a book until she was fourteen years old. After she excavated *Ichthyosaurus*, a neighbor woman gifted her that book—a precious geology book—to encourage Mary's passion. Mary read it over and over, transcribed its words to commit them to memory, and spent long hours redrawing the illustrations by hand.

While Georges Cuvier had the full force of professional science behind him, Mary had herself. Georges had an army of protégés, influence in society, and access to every fossil collection in the world. Mary had the crumbling cliffs of Lyme Regis. As her biographer, Shelley Emling, described it, "In Mary's world, there were few books to open, few discussions to engage in, no lectures to attend, and not even one museum to visit."[6]

Mary, plainly and simply, did not have access to professional paleontology. She was a woman who was poor and lived hand to mouth in the backwaters of England. But she was also smart and resourceful and curious about the world around her. She had intrinsic advantages. These advantages, coupled with her undeniable disadvantages, made it so that she approached the whole subject matter differently.

She wasn't invested in paleontology as a discipline. She hardly knew it *was* a discipline. Mary cared about her finds. She worked in pursuit of her curios—her objects of wonder and awe. She didn't start up in the world of ideas and theories. She started on the ground, digging in the dirt. Georges Cuvier had a vast breadth of knowledge, but Mary Anning had specificity. She was interested in what *that thing* was. He approached from the top and she from the bottom. And, it turned out, natural science needed both approaches to evolve.

༄ ༄ ༄

Mary had, at best, a tenuous feedback loop with the fossil collectors of her day, but she'd heard enough feedback about

Ichthyosaurus to know that it was important. This intensified her curiosity to know what else was hidden in the rocks around her. She entered a period of ravenous collection in her late teens, going out to the cliffs nearly every single day, oftentimes at the peril of her life.

To excavate an eroding cliff is to dance with danger. Mary had to avoid high tide yet closely follow the rainstorms to see what they had exposed. The best time to make finds—the wet winter season—was also the most geologically unstable. On one outing, Mary came within inches of death when a sudden landslide struck and killed her black-and-white terrier, Tray. She wrote to a friend of the incident: "Perhaps you will laugh when I say that the death of my old faithful dog quite upset me, the cliff fell upon him and killed him in a moment before my eyes, and close to my feet, it was but a moment between me and the same fate."[7]

Despite these dangers, Mary continued to scour. In the winter of 1823, at age twenty-four, she made her next major discovery. She found the first complete skeleton of an ancient marine reptile that boasted a big turtle-like body and an extraordinarily long neck. While *Ichthyosaurus* had been undeniably weird, it wasn't totally unlike modern dolphins and porpoises. But this creature, which came to be called *Plesiosaurus*, was so unlike anything alive at the time that many professional scientists thought the fossil was fake.

The question of *Plesiosaurus*'s authenticity eventually went all the way to the top—to the desk of Georges Cuvier himself. At the behest of his peers, Georges reviewed some cursory drawings of the fossil and determined that no, this creature could not be real. It's head-to-neck-to-body proportions were impossible.

That should have been the end of the discussion. Cuvier said no, so it was no. "To the scientific community," Shelley Emling wrote, "Cuvier was far too good at what he did to be wrong . . . He was the kind of authority who never had to prove anything; in this case, just his expressions of doubt were enough to cast a shadow over Mary's discovery. If he was dubious, then everyone else would be too."[8]

Fortunately, one scientific insider dared to push back. His name was William Conybeare, and he was a member of the Geological Society of London. He'd been to Lyme Regis and had seen the fossil for himself. He was sure it was real. So, he asked Mary to draw up a complete set of anatomical illustrations of *Plesiosaurus*. She did, and William called a special meeting of the Geological Society so Georges Cuvier could review the illustrations himself. Mary was not invited. But her illustrations spoke for themselves, and upon closer review, Georges admitted he had rushed to judgement. *Plesiosaurus* was real, he declared, and it was, in his words, "the most amazing creature ever discovered."[9]

With Georges's stamp of approval, *Plesiosaurus* became evidence for extinction that the scientific community could not ignore. It was the first creature to give natural scientists serious pause; it swayed the majority of paleontologists to the belief that many ancient species had indeed gone extinct. Charles Darwin himself wrote extensively about *Plesiosaurus* in 1838, right around the time he formulated his theory of natural selection. When he published *On the Origin of Species* in 1859, he credited both *Plesiosaurus* and *Ichthyosaurus* for helping him develop his theory.

Until her death from breast cancer at age forty-seven, Mary continued to discover some of science's most important specimens. She found the first pterosaur (the ancient flying reptile we now call pterodactyl) in Britain, as well as the first *Squaloraja*, a Jurassic-era fish that shows the missing link between sharks and rays. She also pioneered the rather unglamorous study of fossilized feces, a line of inquiry that eventually allowed paleontologists to reconstruct what ancient animals ate.

Mary was rarely credited for her work in her lifetime. But the trail of documents leading from museums to gentlemen collectors to Mary Anning is well preserved, so today we know a great deal about what she did. In 2010, the Royal Society named her one of the ten most influential British female scientists of all time.[10] Her specimens are on permanent display at Britain's Natural History Museum, and on its website, the museum calls her "the greatest fossil hunter ever known."[11]

Mary's unquenchable curiosity drove her to overcome many obstacles: her dangerous work environment, the social expectations for someone like her, and the professional establishment's refusal to ever include her.

Or perhaps it's not right to say she *overcame* these obstacles. It's more like she walked around them.

She saw them there—the tall towers of prestige with no doors or windows open to her. She saw them and walked around them, on the outside. She roamed beside them, poked at the earth beneath them, looked behind them, and found valuable things scattered all around. She found valuable things right there on the ground—things the people in those towers couldn't see from way up there.

If Jonathon Keats is the mental wanderer, then Mary Anning was the literal wanderer. She was on a random walk of her own—this one not in her imagination but upon the Earth. She was called out into nature every day by her curiosity, on a journey to find who knows what. Important things, to be sure, but nothing she could have faintly imagined before she started.

AMATEURS AND PROFESSIONALS

Now, an admission. I decided long ago that Mary Anning would be the last amateur profiled in this book. That's because she's my favorite. She's my personal hero of amateurism. She's my hero not because she contributed so much to science (which she did) but because she exemplifies the kind of greatness that thrives outside professional circles—the oxymoronic greatness of the master amateur: untrained yet disciplined, unpredictable yet consistent, crude *and* important.

Her example provides a counterbalance to the example of Georges Cuvier—the man we already know to admire. He's the archetype of all the qualities we already know how to value: expertise, reputability, power, and refinement. Mary, on the other hand, is the archetype of all the qualities we've devalued for a long time—at great cost to us all—and are just now realizing that we need to resuscitate. These are grit, resourcefulness, pursuit of interest without transactional reward, and an indomitable determination to do what one wants to do. Not to mention self-reliance, free-range learning, and a fearless willingness to peruse the unknown.

If people had known about Mary Anning in her time, she could have shown them an alternative (and most importantly, an *equal* alternative) set of qualities to admire. But in my opinion, we can't really blame the people of her time for disregarding her. We can blame them for their prejudicial treatment of her. But the whole era in which she lived was moving in a certain direction. It was moving away from the amateur and toward the professional. In nineteenth-century England, everyone was plenty gritty. Everyone had to be scrappy and resourceful to survive. So, those who could afford it looked for ways to become more refined.

But today, in twenty-first-century America, I think we can agree we've all become a little too refined. We've become thin-skinned; we've smoothed out our rough edges to the point where we now feel like any minor chip ruins the whole thing. This keeps us in hot pursuit of perfection, acceptance, credibility, and validity. But look at Mary Anning. She was imperfect, unaccepted, incredible, and invalid. And look at what she did.

In my opinion, going forward, we need to find a balance between the refined and the gritty—between the professional and the master amateur. Each community has something to teach the other. Both communities have gifts to share, and the future will call for them both.

So, I'm not saying we no longer need any Georges Cuviers. We just need Mary Annings too. We need both and should encourage both. No longer should we prop up professionals and put down amateurs; the time when we exclusively exalted professionals and disparaged amateurs is over. Starting now, amateurs are our heroes too.

CHAPTER 11
A MASTER AMATEUR IN TEN METAPHORS

*In the beginner's mind there are many possibilities;
in the expert's mind there are few.*
—Shunryu Suzuki

At the end of a book like this one, every author wants to provide her reader a summary or simplified version of what's been discussed throughout. This is often done by distilling principles or precepts—by offering the reader a road map or a ten-point plan to (in this case) becoming a master amateur.

I have a feeling that, for those of you who now identify as a master amateur, an ending that presents you with a template or list of principles would not be very cogent. The sheer diversity of approaches, motivations, and outcomes presented in this book should show you there's no one way. If I know you at all, I know that you'll want to come up with your own system by which to live and work. You'll want to develop your own set of principles and make your own plan (or lack thereof) for being whomever you want to be and doing whatever you want to do.

So, in lieu of a summary or road map, I will leave you with ten metaphors by which to remember the lessons our exemplar master amateurs have taught us. Some will echo ideas we've already discussed, some will be new, and one very special one is borrowed from an outside source. I'm hopeful these metaphors—these images—are vivid enough to linger with you after you're done reading, memorable enough that you can recall them down the road, and fluid enough that you can make of them whatever you will.

1: THE AMATEUR'S WORMHOLE

An amateur who succeeds has a certain temporal superpower. He is able to bend time and space to see the long-term value of his efforts while those efforts are still undeveloped, unsophisticated, and unimpressive. He can see the vision of a great end-result while his project, business, or invention is still in its early stage—while it is still not very good. He's able to travel through a type of amateur's wormhole, through which he can see and feel the value of his work in the beginning as if he were at the end.

This superpower allows him to tolerate the severely lacking early versions of his work. Early versions of a project, a business, or an invention always have glaring inadequacies. Without a way to deal with them, these inadequacies provide ample evidence for why he should just give up. The wormhole helps him to see that these inadequacies are not the result of a personal failing. They're the result of the reality that nothing starts completed.

So, at the start of every new journey, a master amateur shrinks the space between where he is now (let's say at true beginner) and where he will be if he keeps going (let's say at wise mentor) by harnessing the massive gravity of acceptance.

He accepts that he does not know what he's doing and that he'll have to rely on process for improvement. He accepts that he can only make insufficient predictions about how his project, his business, or his invention will play out. He accepts his shortcomings (some of which may be permanent) as well as his subject-matter ignorance (much of which is temporary). This acceptance propels an amateur past bad, into good, and on to great if he lets it.

2: THE DISPLAY WINDOW

The professional paradigm has played a trick on you. It has tricked you into believing that only your professional expertise is worth something to others. At the extreme, it's convinced you that if you don't have a set of initials after your name, you have very little of value in your possession—you have very little for which anyone would want to compensate you.

This is misdirection; this is an untruth told so that you, the capable amateurs, won't siphon away what the professionals perceive as their exclusive right to high earnings.

So, now, redirect yourself toward a different belief. Believe that you have many things to contribute to the world and that you should be paid for them. Identify and invent innovative revenue streams all around you. Everything you have is potentially worth something to someone. Think about your innate abilities, your acquired skills, your perspective, your physical capacity, your compassion for others, your time and energy—these are all your products, if you choose to sell them.

You also have a valuable expertise from which you can profit, just like the professionals do. That expertise is amateurism: the art of starting anew.

In a way, it's like every master amateur opens their own metaphorical storefront. In the display window of their store, a master amateur arranges all their products: their words, their creations, their experiences, their insights. Anything and everything gets a spot in the window. Even the ability to conjure saleable goods out of nothing is a saleable skill that gets a spot in the window.

And most importantly, a great master amateur keeps their display window sparkling clean. They routinely wipe the glass clean of dust, grime, and any obfuscating factors. This ensures complete transparency. They profit from their products, and they profit, perhaps even more so, from the great commercial advantage known as transparency.

3: ATLAS REPS

One of the beautiful things about being a master of amateurism is that you don't have a readily coherent career story to lose, so you're freer than professionals are to pivot when the impulse strikes you. In fact, the more you pivot from one thing to another, the more interesting your career story becomes. One might even say pivoting *is* your career story.

This makes one particular type of work more doable for you than it is for other people. That is, the difficult, personally draining work of trying to heal the ills of this world.

It is a rare and courageous human who can spend their whole life addressing environmental atrocities, social injustices, and the like. For most of us, this work is too backbreaking to do all the time, for all time.

Luckily, because you are professional pivoters, you master amateurs can take on this type of work when you feel you should—when the need presents itself—without having to do it forever. You can take the weight of the world on your back for a time and then put it back down and do something else. This makes the weight of responsibility not such a great burden; it keeps you from becoming like Atlas—the one punished to shoulder the world for eternity.

Instead, these temporary pivots toward social good are like weight training. They are responsibility reps—Atlas reps.

To gain strength, you must pick up something heavy. But you must also put it down. So, pick up the world for a time, hold it, gain muscle, and then put it back down. This way you'll get stronger. And the next time you see an injustice and think, *Someone needs to do something about that,* you'll be strong enough to tackle it—for a time—yourself.

4: THE BACKPACK CAREER

A wise woman once told me that not making a choice is also a choice. For a master amateur, not making a commitment is also a commitment. Not making a commitment—to one company, one industry, one job function—is making a different kind of commitment: to maintaining a portable career.

We know that our contemporary work landscape is a wilderness. In a wilderness, most people seek shelter; they aim to find a safe home base. This is what full-time positions represent to most people. But a master amateur can take a different approach to dealing with the wilderness. She can pack up everything she needs and go travel—go explore the wilderness. Along the way, she'll gather many more resources and gain many more survival skills than she would working indoors.

By making no commitments and swearing no allegiances, you can go places other people can't go. When you have a self-contained career, you can throw it on your back and take it wherever you wish. Only when your luggage is light can you move freely.

In pursuit of a backpack career, you'll likely sacrifice the safety of a home base. But you will gain something else: choice. You'll gain a sense of control over your life and work. You'll also gain freedom. And what's the point of freelancing if you're not *free*?

You can still fit all the essentials you need inside your backpack career. For a start, you can fit the skills of amateurism. You can fit learning how to learn, adapting to new environments, and recruiting collaborators along the way. You can also fit the knowledge of how much you *don't* know, and with this essential in tow, you'll likely never stop exploring.

5: A COMPLEX MACHINE

For a moment, think of a vocation in a new way. A vocation is not an achievement or an identity or a set of duties. Instead, a vocation is a complex machine that one can construct out of any number of simple machines. By *simple machines*, I mean one's discrete interests, skills, experiences, and passions.

These simple machines, engineered just so, do things together that they cannot do apart. They do *more* together than they could ever do apart. A complex machine is indeed more than the sum of its parts.

Let me give you a hypothetical. Let's say you're a product manager at a biotech startup. As an undergrad, you studied political science. You are deeply concerned about (what you see as) bombs buried within our economic system, the most dangerous one being income inequality. And in your free time, you're learning to code and reading about negotiation tactics.

These may all seem like disparate parts of you—just the multiple facets that any multifaceted person has. But they are also your simple machines, and they are prime for construction. Product management could be the wedge that keeps opportunities open to you. Coding and skillful negotiation could be your lever and pulley—your tactical skills. Your passionate economic concerns could be the gears that keep your mind churning for possible solutions.

Working together, these parts comprise your complex machine. Your complex machine will generate momentum in the direction of your fullest, most abundant vocation. It may click together for you a way in which technology could solve an economic problem. It may move you to see negotiation as a product or income as a service. It may push you to take that run at public office. Whatever direction it moves you in, your complex machine will generate all the motivation you need.

6: AN UPRIGHT LAYMAN

The majority of this book is focused on distilling the principles that successful amateurs have to teach the rest of us—including the professionals among us. But there's one indispensable principle that professionals have to teach amateurs. It's a principle that amateurs should incorporate into everything they do. It is the principle of *acting professionally*.

We know what *being* a professional means. It means having met a given profession's status quo. But *acting* professionally is something different. It's a set of behaviors that anyone can have; it's a manner of being in which you are true to your word, sincere in your actions, responsible with your claims, and considerate of others. There's no reason to think you must meet a profession's status quo before you can adopt these behaviors. Anyone can be an amateur can still act professionally.

In a way, it pains me to even call this principle "acting professionally," because comporting oneself in a trustworthy manner has nothing to do with degrees or certifications or titles. There are no prerequisite courses to being honorable.

It's too bad that trustworthiness and the professions got conflated in the twentieth century, because before then, trustworthiness was a universal standard for all people. In a time before paperwork, a person's word was their bond. Honor applied to everyone. Long before the advent of the modern university and the professions, everyone aimed to be an "upright layman."

Ironically, some level of basic interpersonal trust has disappeared with the rise of the professions. The professional elite's claim over honor had a side effect: it made everyone outside the professions feel less required to follow basic social tenets, like "my word is my bond." My hope is that the rise of the master amateurs helps reverse this effect. I hope it shows everyone that *everyone* should behave like an upright layman.

7: SOUL GEMS

In the world today, there are two types of work. The first type is work that one does to survive: to pay for shelter, provisions—to gain a foothold, financially. Most everyone does this type of work, and because it is so commonplace, many people think it's the only work there is.

A master amateur knows there's also a second type of work. This is the work that one does because one loves it. *Work*, in this case, stands for "love in action." It's shorthand for "love made manifest through effort." When performing this work, a master amateur transforms into the original praiseworthy amateur. *Amator*, "lover of."

Survival-work and love-work may overlap sometimes, but they are elementally different. They are different in their substance. Survival-work comes at you from the outside. Even when you seek it out, you're seeking it out because of external factors—because you need worldly necessities. In this way, survival-work is like wind and water. It erodes from the outside. It's not *bad*, just like wind and water are not *bad*. It's just liable to wear you down.

Love-work, on the other hand, is like fire burning within. It fuels from the inside; it generates heat and pressure that, eventually, have to be released. But while the pressure inside you is still building, the conditions become right for the creation of soul gems: your precious, innate, organic loves.

While your soul is still hot, mix in imagination, adventure, beauty, and mystery. These ingredients, under the right conditions, form the loves on which you'll base your love-work. Everyone has them—these natural loves formed in the crucible of the soul. To become a master amateur, mine your soul for them, now.

8: BEGINNER'S MIND

Shunryu Suzuki, a Zen Buddhist master, once said, "If your mind is empty, it is always ready for anything; it is open to everything. In the beginner's mind there are many possibilities; in the expert's mind there are few."[1]

At the beginning of this chapter, I mentioned that one of these concluding metaphors would be borrowed from an outside source. That metaphor is beginner's mind. Beginner's mind is a concept originating in Zen Buddhism to describe the immense cognitive benefits of knowing that you don't know. To the devoted, it also describes the spiritual progress made when one humbly admits their ignorance. When I tell people I'm writing a book about the upside of amateurism, many of them respond, "Oh, you mean like beginner's mind."

Indeed, the two notions are analogous. One way to envision a master amateur is to say she *acts professionally* with a *beginner's mind*.

Both Zen Buddhism and master amateurism insist that preconceptions limit possibilities. Therefore, beginner's mind is for beginners, but it is also for experts. Amateurism is for amateurs, but it's also for professionals. The more you advance—the more you learn—the more important it becomes to remember your ignorance.

Because ignorance is not stupidity or ineptitude. Ignorance is expansion. *Not knowing* makes *all knowing* available to you. When you have *no thought, all thoughts* are accessible. All roads remain open to one with an empty, ready mind.

9: THE LINE IN THE SAND

In recent years, I've spoken to many people who think amateurism is the future—who see the beauty in a life of perpetual novicehood. However, not one of those people wants an amateur to perform their heart surgery or lay the foundation for their house. Myself included. Amateurism is an expertise in and of itself, but it's not the *only* expertise society needs. We need single-subject experts too, to perform highly specialized tasks that it simply would not be right for an amateur to perform.

So, the question becomes, where is the line in the sand? At what point does an amateur overstep the boundaries of suitability and attempt to do something he or she should not do?

I've come to believe that the line is not around any particular industry. Even in the ultraprofessional industries of law, medicine, and academia, there are places where it's appropriate for amateurs to participate.

Instead, I think the line is drawn around activities that you need to get right on the first try. If not getting it right on the first try would be a disaster—if it would bring harm to you or others—then don't just go try without knowing what will happen. Learn from a credible source what you need to know before you begin. Train, practice, get supervised, get credentialed, and be a professional.

But notice, if you will, the vast number of activities that this criterion still leaves open to the amateur. Any pursuit that allows for a second or third try—any pursuit that might even *benefit* from multiple tries—is open to the amateur. Anything that evolves, any pursuit where process improves the outcome, is on the amateur's side of the line in the sand. These are the miles and miles of sandy beaches on which an amateur can play.

10: THE SEASHORE

As we settle down into the twenty-first century, the great divide that's separated amateurs from professionals for the last hundred years is not so great anymore. Aside from the line in the sand, which I believe still holds firm, the distinction between what's amateur and what's professional is softening by the day.

Ideologically, amateurs are inching toward becoming more professional. They're setting high standards for themselves and taking the work they do seriously (no matter how traditionally unqualified they are to do it). This seriousness is why we call ourselves master amateurs and not just amateurs.

The professional world, in turn, is starting to crack open its doors to amateurism. MBA programs teach that a good business leader must maintain beginner's mind. Postgraduate science programs teach that citizen scientists working en masse can accomplish incredible things. Medical students are now taught to collaborate with a patient on their treatment plan instead of dictating one down from on high.

Even within individual people, the distinction is softening. I predict that many people who read this book will identify as both a professional *and* a master amateur, making the distinction meaningless, at least for them.

So, going forward, what separates the two—the master amateur from the professional—will not be a great divide. It will be a fluid, oscillating frontier. It will be like the border between the sand and the sea. Always in motion, never totally clear. On some days, the line that divides will be a little more this way. Other days, it will be a little more that way. Sometimes the tide will be higher; sometimes it will be lower. But it will always be moving across common ground.

And just as the tide and the sand are made of different stuff, destined to negotiate a constantly shifting dividing line, they are also something bigger together. Together, they are a seashore. They comprise something bigger, more beautiful, and more powerful, together. They are two, but when you zoom out, you can see they are also one.

NOTES

CHAPTER 1

1. Elizabeth B. Keeney, *The Botanizers: Amateur Scientists in Nineteenth-Century America* (Chapel Hill, NC: University of North Carolina Press, 1992).
2. Magali Sarfatti Larson, *The Rise of Professionalism: Monopolies of Competence and Sheltered Markets* (Berkeley, CA: University of California Press, 1977), 52.
3. Philippa Levine, *The Amateur and the Professional: Antiquarians, Historians and Archaeologists in Victorian England 1838–1886* (Cambridge, UK: Cambridge University Press, 1986), 23.
4. John Quiggin, "Start with the Household," in *Amateur Media: Social, Cultural and Legal Perspectives*, ed. Dan Hunter, Ramon Lobato, Megan Richardson, and Julian Thomas (New York: Routledge, 2013), 29.
5. Julia Evetts, "The Concept of Professionalism: Professional Work, Professional Practice and Learning," in *International Handbook of Research in Professional and Practice-Based Learning*, ed. Stephen Billett, Christian Harteis, and Hans Gruber (New York: Springer, 2014), 34.

CHAPTER 2

1. https://nextviewventures.com/blog/hbs-startup-unicorns/

2. https://insights.stackoverflow.com/survey/2016#work
3. https://www.amazon.co.uk/Go-Against-Flow-Entrepreneurship-Success/dp/1910692514
4. https://www.ted.com/talks/reshma_saujani_teach_girls_bravery_not_perfection
5. https://www.nytimes.com/1992/03/05/garden/great-hello-mystery-is-solved.html
6. http://content.time.com/time/subscriber/article/0,33009,947523-1,00.html; http://edisonmuseum.org/content3399.html
7. https://edison.rutgers.edu/newsletter9.html
8. https://edison.rutgers.edu/newsletter9.html
9. https://www.fastcompany.com/59549/failure-doesnt-suck
10. https://www.vice.com/en_us/article/78xqjx/10-years-ago-today-youtube-launched-as-a-dating-website
11. https://www.theguardian.com/books/2014/apr/04/carrie-stephen-king-horror
12. http://web.archive.org/web/20060316221021/http:/www.jkrowling.com/textonly/en/extrastuff_view.cfm?id=1
13. https://www.smithsonianmag.com/history/george-washington-the-reluctant-president-49492/
14. https://founders.archives.gov/documents/Washington/04-05-02-0316
15. https://founders.archives.gov/GEWN-04-05-02-0388

CHAPTER 3

1. https://www.youtube.com/watch?v=Np3srx0nAZI
2. http://www.pewresearch.org/fact-tank/2017/05/16/todays-young-workers-are-more-likely-than-ever-to-have-a-bachelors-degree/
3. https://www.usatoday.com/story/money/2017/01/13/millennials-falling-behind-boomer-parents/96530338/
4. https://www.patreon.com/
5. https://www.upwork.com/about/
6. http://www.nydailynews.com/entertainment/8-weird-people-money-fiverr-article-1.2438065

7. http://www.whattheheck.com/ebay/meaninglife.html
8. https://wanderingaimfully.com/about/
9. http://usatoday30.usatoday.com/money/advertising/2005-01-25-forehead_x.htm
10. Quiggin, "Start with the Household," 29.
11. https://www.consumerreports.org/food/meal-delivery-services-put-dinner-on-your-doorstep/
12. https://github.com/ConfuddledPenguin/CS412---Wall-Street-Journal-Searcher/blob/master/Split%20Files/WSJ_0801/WSJ_0801.033
13. https://www.orau.org/ptp/collection/quackcures/radith.htm
14. https://www.orau.org/ptp/collection/quackcures/radith.htm
15. https://academic.oup.com/jnci/article-abstract/82/21/1667/927947?redirectedFrom=PDF
16. https://www.catholicnewsagency.com/news/bizarre-details-emerge-as-fake-priest-gets-busted-in-la-80065
17. https://www.catholicnewsagency.com/news/bizarre-details-emerge-as-fake-priest-gets-busted-in-la-80065
18. https://www.theguardian.com/artanddesign/2014/apr/22/forged-art-scandal-new-york-artist-china-spain

CHAPTER 4

1. http://www.wsmv.com/story/16690408/local-woman-fights-to-solve-friends-cold-case-murder
2. I Solved a Murder, "Sheila Wysocki," directed by Evan Cecil, written by Greg Sirota, featuring Katrina Sherwood, Kurt Cotton, and Evangeline Crittenden, aired February 24, 2013, on USA, https://www.imdb.com/title/tt2740920/.
3. https://www.cnn.com/2018/05/18/health/teens-write-gun-legislation-trnd/index.html
4. https://coloradoboulevard.net/preventing-gun-violence-resolution-by-alhambra-students/
5. http://kuow.org/post/13-kids-sue-washington-state-life-liberty-and-livable-climate

6. https://www.cnn.com/2018/05/22/health/utah-students-climate-change-trnd/index.html
7. http://www.ladybugfoundation.ca/who-we-are/hannah-taylor-founder/
8. http://www.sun-sentinel.com/news/education/fl-reg-teen-nonprofits-20171101-story.html#
9. https://gizmodo.com/meet-the-oregon-middle-schoolers-fighting-for-net-neutr-1823781219
10. Clara Barton, *The Story of My Childhood* (Meriden, CT: Journal Press, 1907), 99–100.
11. Elizabeth Brown Pryor, Clara Barton, *Professional Angel* (Philadelphia: University of Pennsylvania Press, 1987), 316.
12. Pryor, Clara Barton, *Professional Angel*, 250.
13. https://redcrosschat.org/2015/07/17/13-reasons-clara-barton-thenewten/
14. https://redcrosschat.org/2015/07/17/13-reasons-clara-barton-thenewten/
15. https://www.nps.gov/clba/learn/historyculture/upload/cbservice.pdf

CHAPTER 5

1. http://www.rolexawards.com/profiles/laureates/forrest_marion_mims_iii/overview
2. https://www.jameco.com/Jameco/workshop/diy/forrest-mims.html
3. http://discovermagazine.com/2008/dec/19-the-amateur-scientists-who-might-cure-cancer-from-their-basements
4. http://americanhistory.si.edu/collections/search/object/nmah_334396
5. https://makezine.com/2016/05/04/classic-circuits-forrest-m-mims-iii/
6. https://features.slashdot.org/story/14/06/08/206220/interviews-forrest-mims-answers-your-questions

7. http://www.arn.org/docs/orpages/or131/mimsrpt3.htm
8. Larson, *Rise of Professionalism*, 231.
9. https://web.archive.org/web/20080302053743/http://www.businessweek.com/bwdaily/dnflash/jul2004/nf20040728_3153_db078.htm
10. Bruce Brooks Pfeiffer, ed., *Frank Lloyd Wright on Architecture, Nature, and the Human Spirit: A Collection of Quotations* (Portland, OR: Pomegranate, 2011), 50.
11. https://franklloydwright.org/site/unity-temple/
12. Biography in sound: https://archive.org/details/BiographiesInSound/1956-08-07NbcBiographiesInSound53MeetFrankLloydWright.mp3
13. Biography in sound: https://archive.org/details/BiographiesInSound/1956-08-07NbcBiographiesInSound53MeetFrankLloydWright.mp3
14. Biography in sound: https://archive.org/details/BiographiesInSound/1956-08-07NbcBiographiesInSound53MeetFrankLloydWright.mp3

CHAPTER 6

1. https://hbr.org/2017/04/why-you-should-have-at-least-two-careers
2. https://hbr.org/2017/04/why-you-should-have-at-least-two-careers
3. Jack Hitt, *Bunch of Amateurs: A Search for the American Character* (New York: Crown, 2012), 34.
4. https://www.biography.com/people/leonardo-da-vinci-40396
5. https://www.fastcompany.com/3056140/why-the-21st-century-economy-needs-more-polymaths
6. http://adsabs.harvard.edu/abs/2003BAAS...35.1472K
7. Gerrit Verschuur, *The Invisible Universe: The Story of Radio Astronomy*, 2nd ed. (New York: Springer, 2007), 14.
8. https://web.archive.org/web/20120227074011/http://jump.cv.nrao.edu/dbtw-wpd/Textbase/Documents/grncr071988b.pdf

9. http://www.thehistoryblog.com/archives/14729
10. https://www.wsj.com/articles/SB10001424127887324900204578286272195339456
11. https://www.wsj.com/articles/SB10001424127887324900204578286272195339456
12. https://hbr.org/ideacast/2017/07/build-your-portfolio-career

CHAPTER 7

1. https://www.vanityfair.com/news/2006/08/loosechange200608
2. https://www.vimooz.com/2017/10/06/7th-catalina-film-festival-awards/
3. https://www.youtube.com/watch?v=hpFNG8DDTrs
4. https://www.youtube.com/watch?v=hpFNG8DDTrs
5. https://www.fastcompany.com/40565190/this-activist-is-still-fighting-to-get-flint-clean-water
6. https://www.youtube.com/watch?v=699wQ_s1hUY
7. https://www.youtube.com/watch?v=699wQ_s1hUY
8. https://www.smithsonianmag.com/innovation/whistleblowers-marc-edwards-and-leeanne-walters-winner-smithsonians-social-progress-ingenuity-award-180961125/
9. https://www.brainyquote.com/quotes/margaret_mead_100502
10. https://www.ted.com/talks/scilla_elworthy_fighting_with_non_violence?language=en

CHAPTER 8

1. http://fortune.com/2018/05/01/americans-lonely-cigna-study/
2. https://www.nextpittsburgh.com/features/why-1-4-million-people-are-following-ali-spagnola/
3. https://www.forbes.com/sites/andyfrye/2018/08/22/how-ali-spagnola-took-fitness-and-comedy-and-became-a-social-media-star/#2351611275a3
4. https://www.dailymail.co.uk/news/article-4532266/75-cent-children-want-YouTubers-vloggers.html

5. https://www.nytimes.com/2018/05/19/style/my-favorite-murder-podcast-murderinos.html
6. https://www.goodreads.com/quotes/8446
7. https://www.today.com/food/15-julia-child-quotes-inspire-wannabe-chef-all-us-t101848
8. https://www.theodysseyonline.com/julia-child-5-insights-into-the-endearing-personality-behind-the-chefs-jacket
9. https://www.goodreads.com/quotes/322262
10. https://kcts9.org/blogs/julia-child-tall-numbers-tall-lady
11. https://www.goodreads.com/quotes/9600
12. http://www.massbroadcastershof.org/hall-of-fame/hall-of-fame-2014/julia-child/
13. Lawrence R. Schehr and Allen S. Weiss, *French Food: On the Table, on the Page, and in French Culture* (New York: Routledge, 2001), 225.
14. https://www.youtube.com/watch?v=VvKIghChhNw

CHAPTER 9

1. https://kinseysicks.com/
2. https://www.cdc.gov/mmwr/preview/mmwrhtml/mm5021a2.htm
3. https://www.salon.com/2000/10/17/drag_queen/
4. https://www.thecrimson.com/article/2018/9/20/ben-schatz-dragapella/
5. https://www.salon.com/2000/10/17/drag_queen/
6. https://kinseysicks.com/
7. https://www.thecrimson.com/article/2018/9/20/ben-schatz-dragapella/
8. http://www.islandnet.com/~see/weather/history/howard.htm
9. Richard Hamblyn, *The Invention of Clouds: How an Amateur Meteorologist Forged the Language of the Skies* (New York: Picador, 2001), 44.
10. Hamblyn, *Invention of Clouds*, 145.
11. Hamblyn, *Invention of Clouds*, 119.

12. http://www.islandnet.com/~see/weather/history/howard.htm; https://www.weatheronline.co.uk/reports/weatherbrains/Luke-Howard.htm
13. Hamblyn, *Invention of Clouds*, 2.
14. Hamblyn, *Invention of Clouds*, 77.
15. Hamblyn, *Invention of Clouds*, 239.
16. Amelia Earhart, *The Fun of It: Random Records of My Own Flying and of Women in Aviation* (New York: Brewer, Warren & Putnam, 1932; Chicago: Academy Chicago Publishers, 2006), 25. Citations refer to Academy Chicago Publishers edition.
17. Earhart, Fun of It, 97.
18. https://www.goodreads.com/quotes/6378366-there-is-more-to-life-than-being-a-passenger
19. Earhart, *Fun of It*, 54.
20. Earhart, *Fun of It*, 96.
21. Earhart, *Fun of It*, title page.
22. Earhart, *Fun of It*, 238.
23. https://www.atlasobscura.com/articles/the-women-who-rose-high-in-the-early-days-of-hot-air-ballooning
24. https://en.wikipedia.org/wiki/Sophie_Blanchard
25. https://www.usatoday.com/story/weather/2015/04/08/david-hoadley-first-storm-chaser-tornadoes/25413937/

CHAPTER 10

1. https://www.sfgate.com/bayarea/article/Aristotle-s-law-petition-confounds-blase-Berkeley-2783321.php
2. https://www.sfgate.com/entertainment/article/Project-Aims-At-Genetically-Engineered-God-SF-3237252.php
3. https://www.newyorker.com/magazine/2010/03/15/plant-tv
4. https://www.goodreads.com/quotes/987
5. http://search.chadpearce.com/Home/BOOKS/8773894-Meaning-of-It-All-by-Feynman-Nobel-Laureate.pdf, 7.

6. Shelley Emling, *The Fossil Hunter: Dinosaurs, Evolution, and the Woman Whose Discoveries Changed the World* (New York: St. Martin's Press, 2009), 51.
7. https://www.famousscientists.org/mary-anning/
8. Emling, *The Fossil Hunter*, 81.
9. https://www.famousscientists.org/mary-anning/
10. https://royalsociety.org/news/2010/influential-british-women/
11. https://www.csmonitor.com/Technology/2014/0521/Google-honors-Mary-Anning-the-greatest-fossil-hunter-ever-known

CHAPTER 11

1. Shunryu Suzuki, *Zen Mind, Beginner's Mind: Informal Talks on Zen Meditation and Practice* (New York: Weatherhill, 1970; Boulder, CO: Shambala, 2011), 2. Citations refer to the Shambala edition.

ACKNOWLEDGMENTS

First and foremost, thank you to the individuals who provided interviews for this book: Dylan Avery, Jonathon Keats, Forrest Mims III, Matt Monahan, Ben Schatz, Kabir Sehgal, Charu Sharma, Ali Spagnola, and Sheila Wysocki. Your stories frame and define what this book is about, and I'm immensely grateful that you chose to share them with me. Thank you to Michelle Tessler of Tessler Literary Agency for providing some critical feedback on an early draft of this book. Thank you to Sharon Hernandez, a wonderful freelancer who came to me via Upwork, for helping me compile a gigantic list of amateurs from history—it was from this list that the book's historical exemplars emerged. Lastly, thank you to Sara Addicott, my production editor at Girl Friday Productions, and to the entire Girl Friday team for helping me bring this book to life.

INDEX

A

Acting professionally, principle of, 207–8
Activism, 136–38
Advertising principles, 41
AIDS crisis, 161, 166
Allen, Paul, 78
AlphaBoost (company), 40
Altair 8800 (computer), 78, 83
Amateur/amateurism (terms):
 definitions, 4–5, 14–16, 167
Amateurism
 as an expertise, 4, 16–17, 203, 210
 core competencies and skills, 6–9
 future role, 16–17, 186, 210
 history, 9–11, 16
 spirit of, 71, 167, 176
 as a vocation, 5
 See also master amateurs
American Institute of Architects (AIA), 91, 93–94
American Red Cross, 72
Andrews Sisters (singing group), 159
Anger, 119, 128–129, 136–38

Anning, Mary, 191–98
Antiquarianism, 13–14
Archaeology
 ancient Roman hairstyles, 113–16
 as professional field, 13–14
Architecture, 5, 91–94
Armchair scholars, 14
Art forgery, 54–55
Artist, conceptual. *see* Monahan, Matt
Askesian Society, 171–72
Assumptions, 181–82, 186
Astronomy, 12, 110–13
Astrophysical Journal, 112
Atmospheric monitoring, 78
Automobile prototypes, 31
Avery, Dylan, 120–28, 130, 151
Aviation, 173–77
Avilez, Abatto, 160–61
Aykroyd, Dan, 153

B

Bailey, William J. A., 51–52, 55
Barton, Clara, 71–75
Battle of Cedar Mountain (1862), 74
Beck, Simone, 154–55

Beginner's mind, 201, 209–11
Bell, Alexander Graham, 29
Bergantiños Díaz, José Carlos, 55
Bertholle, Louisette, 154–55
Bharara, Preet, 55
Billings, Patricia, 31
Blanchard, Sophie, 177
Blind people, 79–80, 82
Botany, history of, 10–12
Branwyn, Gareth, 83
British Isles: volcanic haze (1783), 169
Brockovich, Erin, 136
Byers, Eben, 52

C
Career trajectories
 diversified, 2–3, 48, 105–6
 linear, 68, 102, 105
Charlatans, 51–57
Child, Julia, 152–57
Child, Paul, 154
Chu, Judy, 70
Citizen scientists, 79, 135–36, 211
Civil War, U.S., 72–74
Climate change, 70
Cloud types, 170–72
Coding, 7–8, 21
Coined: The Rich Life of Money and How Its History Has Shaped Us (Sehgal), 98–99, 103
Cold cases, 65–66
College, 12–13, 47, 87, 94–95
Commodification, 47–49
Computer kit, build-it-yourself, 78
Conspiracy theories, 120, 126, 130
Constitutional Convention (1787), 34
Conybeare, William, 197
Cooking, 152–57
Corruption, 48, 51
Creationism, 84–85

Creative constraints, 95–96
Criminal investigation, 62–66
Crowdfunding platforms, 48
Cuban, Mark, 126
Curie, Marie, 51
Curiosity, 186–89
Cuvier, Georges, 193–97, 199
Cyanobacteria, 181

D
Dallas Police Department (DPD), 60, 62–65, 75
Darwin, Charles, 84, 197
Deforestation, 70–71
DNA testing, 62–63, 65
Documentary films, 21, 24, 120–27, 184
Drag performances, 159–68
Duhamel, Albert, 152
Dyson, James, 31

E
Earhart, Amelia, 173–77
Edison, Thomas, 28–31, 37, 91
Edwards, Marc, 134
Electronics guidebooks, 77–78, 83
Elworthy, Scilla, 138
Emling, Shelley, 195–97
Environmental issues, 70–71
Esoteric products, 46, 57
Ethics, code of, 129–32
Evetts, Julia, 16
Evolution, theory of, 84–85, 90
Experimental philosophers, 180
Experimentation, 3, 31, 36, 189
Extinct species, 193–94, 197

F
Fallingwater (house), Pennsylvania, 91–92
Faraday, Michael, 1, 189–91
Feynman, Richard, 190

Filmmaking, 21, 24, 120–27, 184
Finance, 101–3
First tries, 33, 210–11
Fischer, Andrew, 49
500 Startups (company), 19–21
Fiverr (website), 48–49
Flat-Earth theorists, 130
Flemma, Tess, 70–71
Flexibility: as survival skill, 3, 116–17
Flint, Michigan: water crisis, 132–35
Ford, Henry, 31
Forged artworks, 54–55
Formal education, 3–4, 20, 78, 90, 92, 131
Fossil collectors, 192–98
Francis, Pope, 53
Francis I, King (France), 109
Franklin, Benjamin, 108–9
The French Chef (TV show), 153
Friedman, Jerry, 160
Future
    core competencies, 6–9, 105–7
    interdisciplinary thinking, 107–8, 116–17
    role of amateurism, 16–17, 186, 210
    survival skills, 3, 116–17, 182
    work trends, 3, 97–98

G
Gandolfini, James, 122
Gates, Bill, 78
Geobond (plaster), 31–32
Getting Started in Electronics (Mims), 78, 83
Globalization, 107
Go Against the Flow (film), 21
God: laboratory experiments, 181
Goins, Jeff, 109
Great Fogg of 1783, 169, 188

Greco-Roman statues, 113
Greed, 39, 45, 47, 51, 55
Guevara, Gary, 54
Guggenheim Museum, New York, New York, 92
Guidelines, ethical, 131
Gun violence, 69–70

H
Hairdo archaeology, 113–16
Hardstark, Georgia, 148–49
Harrison, Benjamin, 34
Harry Potter books, 32–33
Hawks, Frank, 173
Henyey, Louis, 112
History, study of, 13–14
Hitt, Jack, 108
HIV, 160–61, 164
Hoadley, David, 177
Honesty, 56–57, 129
Honor, 207–8
Hot-air ballooning, 177
Howard, Luke, 169–73, 176
Howard, Robert, 172

I
Ichthyosaurus, 193, 196–97
Ignorance, acceptance of, 129, 180–81, 203, 209–10
Imperfection, comfort with, 24, 28, 36–37
Independent learning, 6–7
Indifference, 27–28
Indoctrination, 90
Influencers, social media, 140, 151
Instagram, 32, 42–43, 45, 48, 140
Institutions, 78, 94–95
Intellectual freedom, 88
Intelligent design, 84
Interdisciplinary thinking, 107–8, 116–17

J

J. P. Morgan (company), 98, 101–2
Jansky, Karl, 110–11
Journalism, 131
Julia Domna, Empress (Roman Empire), 113, 115–16

K

Karim, Jawed, 32
Kasky, Cameron, 69
Keats, Jonathon, 179–87, 190, 198
Keenan, Philip, 112
Keller, Irwin, 160
Kelly, Maurice, 160
Kerry, John, 100
Kilgariff, Karen, 148–49
King, Stephen, 32
Kinsey, Alfred, 160
Kinsey Sicks (theatrical group), 160–66
Knoedler & Company (art gallery), 54–55
Knowledge, decentralization of, 7, 107, 150

L

Larson, Magali Sarfatti, 12, 85
Lead poisoning, 133–34
Learning, independent, 7
Leeuwenhoek, Antonie van, 31
Leisure, man of, 1–2, 9–10, 171
Leonardo da Vinci, 108–9
Levine, Philippa, 14
Light bulbs, 29
Light-emitting diodes, 80–81
Loose Change (film), 120–21, 123–27
Los Angeles, California
 art installation, 43–44
 Ennis House, 92
 priest impersonator, 53–54
 selfie murals, 43

Los Angeles, California (*cont.*)
 student-drafted gun referendum, 69–70
Love: spirit of amateurism, 167, 176
Love-work, 167–69, 208–9
Luce, Henry, 94
Lyme Regis, England, 191–93, 195, 197

M

Mallory, Walter S., 30
Marsalis, Wynton, 100
Mass shootings, 69
Master (term): definition, 5
Master amateurs
 activism, 136–38
 career trajectories, 2–3, 48, 105–6
 code of ethics, 129–32
 comfort with imperfection, 24, 28, 36–37
 core competencies, 6–9, 75, 95–96, 105, 169
 definition of term, 3–6
 freedom vs. security, 88–90
 impulses, 6, 67–68, 169
 interdisciplinary thinking, 107–8, 116–17
 personal brands, 146–47, 156
 philosophy, 3–4
 pivoting, 68, 204–5
 profit making, 47–51, 56–57, 203
 rise of, 2–4, 208
 self-centeredness, 11, 68, 75
 work and identity, 24, 45
McClelland, Robert, 72
McClure, Dave, 19–20
Mead, Margaret, 136–37
Meal-delivery services, 50
Medical professionals, 73–75
Mena, Erwin "Padre," 53–55
Meteorology, 170–72, 176

Meyers, Joseph, 94
Microbiology, 31
Microsoft, 78
Midler, Bette, 159
Mims, Forrest, III, 77–87, 90, 95, 151
MITS (company), 78, 83
Model Rocketry (magazine), 83
Monahan, Matt, 39–48, 57, 65, 104, 145
Money
 and corruption, 48, 51
 finance, 101–3
 profit making, 47–51, 56–57
 revenue streams, 47, 203
 vs. time, 104
Murals, selfie, 43
Murders
 cold case, 59–66
 podcast, 148–49
Music and musicians
 a cappella drag quartet, 160
 "one-gal band," 139, 142
 Wall Street music producer, 98, 100, 102
My Favorite Murder (podcast), 148–49

N
Natural science, 10–11, 195
Natural selection, theory of, 85, 197
Nature (journal), 78, 87, 90
Neo-goods and services, 48–49, 57
Net neutrality, 71
New York, New York
 art forgery scandal, 54–55
 financial sector, 101
 museum, 92
 September 11 attacks, 120
Next Play (startup), 20–21
Nichols, Marden, 115

O
Obligate amateurs, 151
Office of Strategic Services (OSS), Washington, D.C., 153–54
$100K (art-object series), 45
Orr, Douglas, 94

P
Paleontology, 194–97
Parabolic dishes, 111
Patreon (crowdfunding platform), 48, 140, 145
Peer-to-peer marketplaces, 48
Pei-Shen Qian, 54–55
Personal brands, 145, 147–51, 156
Philosophy, study of, 183
Phonograph, invention of, 28–29
Pico-Union (neighborhood), Los Angeles, California, 43–44
Piel, Jonathan, 84, 86
Pilots, female: world records, 175
Pivoting, 32, 68, 204–5
Plants
 amateur botanists, 10–13
 movies theaters for, 184–85
Plaster, 31–32
Plesiosaurus, 196–97
Podcasts, 32, 148–49
Polymaths, 108–9, 116
Popular Electronics (magazine), 78, 83
Portfolio careers, 98–100, 102–5, 108
Powell, Julie, 156
Preconceptions, 210
Priest impersonator, 53–54
Private investigators, 63–66
Profession/professional (terms): definitions, 15–16
Professional organizations, 88–90

Professionals
    behavior, 207–8
    elite status, 2, 208
    expertise, 2, 203, 210
    society's need for, 210
    status quo, 16, 90, 207
    vs. amateurs, 4, 9–17, 27, 198–200, 210–12
    work tasks, 168
Profiteering, 51, 54
Prototypes, 30–31
Pryor, Elizabeth Brown, 73–74

Q
Qian, Pei-Shen, 54–55
Quantum entanglement, 181

R
Radar technology, 80
Radiation poisoning, 52
Radio astronomy, 110–12, 117
RadioShack books, 77–78, 83, 86
Radithor (health tonic), 51–52
Rain forests, 70–71, 78
Reber, Grote, 110–13, 117
Relationships, for-profit, 48, 50
Renaissance men, 108–9
Rivers, Pitt, 14
Roberts, Ed, 83
Robie, Frederick and Lora, 93
Robie House, Chicago, Illinois, 93–94
Rockets, model, 79, 82–83
Romans, ancient: hairstyles, 114–15
Rosales, Glafira, 55
Rowe, Korey, 121, 123–24, 126
Rowling, J. K., 32–33

S
Saint Ignatius of Loyola, Highland Park, California, 53
Samota, Angie, 59–66
San Francisco, California
    cafés, 22, 179
    Castro district, 161
    concert, 159
    startup event, 19–20
Saujani, Reshma, 24
Schatz, Ben, 159–68
Schwab, Armand, Jr., 84–85
Scientific American (magazine), 84, 86
Sehgal, Kabir, 98–105, 107, 117, 164–65
Self-centeredness, 11, 68, 75
Self-righteousness, 75
"Selfie" phenomenon, 43
September 11 attacks (9/11), 119–24, 128
Shanksville, Pennsylvania, 120, 124
Sharma, Charu, 20–26, 28, 45, 65, 141
Side-hustles, 3, 97, 102, 105–6
Silicon Valley (region), California, 20–21, 44
Sky & Telescope (magazine), 112
Sky maps, 112
Snook, Neta, 174
Snyder, Rick, 132
Social media, 140–49, 151
Software engineers, 20
Southern Methodist University, Dallas, Texas, 60–61
Spagnola, Ali, 139–46, 150–51, 157
Sparks, Virgil, 62
Specialization, 106–7, 116, 210
Startups, 19–21, 32
Status quos, 16, 36, 88–91, 96, 182, 207
Stephens, Janet, 113–16
Storm chasing, 177
Struve, Otto, 112
Survival-work, 208–9
Suzuki, Shunryu, 201, 209

T
Taylor, Hannah, 70
Technical skills, 7–8
Teenagers, 69–71
Telescopes, 12, 111
The Terror Timeline (catalog), 123
Texas Instruments, 80–81
Thompson, Paul, 123
Thought experiments, 180, 183
Time vs. money, 104
TMFA (The Most Famous Artist). *see* Monahan, Matt
Transatlantic flights, 173, 175–76
Transparency, 39, 57, 137, 204
Trial and error, 7, 20, 31
True-crime stories, 148–49
Trustworthiness, 207–8
Truther movement, 123–24
Tsai, Christine, 20
Twitter, 32, 140

U
Unity Temple, Oak Park, Illinois, 92–93
Upright laymen, 207–8
U.S. Constitution, 34–35

V
Vacuum tubes, 81–82
Venice Beach, Los Angeles, California, 43
Vietnam, 82
Vocations, 5, 106, 206–7

W
Wabi-sabi (art principle), 36
Wall Street, New York, New York, 101
Walling, Dayne, 133
Walters, LeeAnne, 132–37
Washington, George, 33–35

Water
  lead contamination, 132–35
  radioactive cure-all, 51–52
Weather observation, 170–72, 177
World Trade Center, New York, New York, 120
Wright, Frank Lloyd, 91–95
Wysocki, Sheila, 59–67, 75, 127–28

Y
YouTube, 32, 124–25, 140, 146

Z
Zen Buddhism, 209–10
Zook, Jason, 49

ABOUT THE AUTHOR

Kira Asatryan is a contributor to *Time* and authors the popular *Psychology Today* blog *The Art of Closeness*, which has garnered over three million views. She is the author of *Stop Being Lonely: Three Simple Steps to Developing Close Friendships and Deep Relationships*—a finalist for the 2016 Books for a Better Life Award and an Amazon #1 New Release. Before writing her first book, Kira worked for ten years in digital marketing for Silicon Valley startups. She is also a certified relationship coach, an aspiring gemologist, and a consummate master amateur.

www.ingramcontent.com/pod-product-compliance
Lightning Source LLC
Chambersburg PA
CBHW020404080526
44584CB00014B/1173